DEPRESSION:
Don't Take It Lying Down

Day to Day Coping Strategies for the Down Hearted

Karen Yochim LPC

Scripture taken from the NEW AMERICAN STANDARD BIBLE Copyright 1960, 1962, 1963, 1968, 1971, 1972, 1973, 1975, 1977, 1995 by the Lockman Foundation. Used by permission.

ISBN: 1478290277
ISBN 13: 9781478290278

Dedicated to anyone who is slogging
through a period of despondency.

IT'S TEMPORARY!

Very special thanks to Barry Fouts. Thanks also to Marilyn Agee, Sharon Sheridan, Pat Wilcox, and all other Psychiatric nurses and Psych workers everywhere, who day and night are helping clients move on through some of the toughest times of their lives.

Thank you also to Hector Fosser, M.D, Twinkle Yochim, Bill Cardy, Anne Ruth, and so many of our friends from high school days who have valiantly survived and bravely overcome harrowing and/or devastating life events. You, old friends, inspire by your spirit and determination to live fully despite what may have come your way.

JANUARY 1

…Why have you been standing here idle all day long?
– Matthew 20: 6

If struggling with depressed mood, we may feel overwhelmed with even the simplest of daily routine tasks. This results in our feeling even worse because of all the tasks we've let slide owing to low energy. However, once we make ourselves begin the chore, momentum takes over, and it's often easier to take a bite out of that job than we thought it would be. If we don't begin the job at all, however, we're not giving momentum a chance to kick in. A big help, if we've been avoiding or stalling, is to keep remembering that venerable law of Physics: A body at rest tends to stay at rest. A body in motion tends to stay in motion.

An achievement today is_____

_____

_____

_____

_____

_____

_____

_____

JANUARY 2

....sorrow has filled your heart.

– John 16: 6

Individuals experiencing a period of depressed feelings may find themselves reviewing painful past experiences repeatedly. This is self-defeating, and conducive to staying stuck in the mire, the swamp, and the rut of depression. One of the ways out of a stalled or stuck phase is to *reframe* or change the way we're looking at our life. We can reframe the past by looking at it as a series of chapters in the novel of our life. When unwelcome thoughts about the past enter our mind, we can remind ourselves: "That's from a chapter I've already read. I'm way past that now, and focused on writing a new chapter."

An achievement today is_____

_____

_____

_____

_____

_____

_____

_____

JANUARY 3

If I do not do the works of My Father, do not believe Me.

– John 10: 37

Who would you like to see starring in the movie of your life? What sort of movie would it be? A big box office extravaganza or a small budget movie or a thriller? A love story or a comedy? Do you like the script so far or do you want to make some changes? Sometimes depression comes out of being dissatisfied with our script. Changes need to be made to the story, the plot. Our inner self wants change, and depressed feelings are a signal for this. Perhaps the signals are warning that we're not utilizing our God given gifts. Have you used your talents in some way today?

My movie so far is a_____

_____

_____

_____

_____

_____

_____

_____

_____

JANUARY 4

...an hour is coming...
– John 16: 25

Sometimes depression has to do with impatience. Things aren't happening fast enough. However, our sense of time is arbitrary and artificial. It has a lot to do with individual perception. For example, when having fun, time passes too quickly. When bored, time slows to a crawl, and we keep looking at our watch. If events aren't happening fast enough for you in your life, you're not taking into account that God's time is totally different than our fragile, misguided perception of it. Relax, and know that things will happen when they're ready to happen. We can enjoy life in the meantime, rather than drum our fingers impatiently while feeling frustrated and depressed. Spinning our wheels won't make things happen any faster.

An achievement today is_____

_____

_____

_____

_____

_____

JANUARY 5

…you will grieve, but your grief will be turned into joy.
– John 16: 20

Grief comes in waves. If you're experiencing grief over a loss, be aware that it ebbs and flows. It may be loss of a job, a friend, or a way of life. Your house may have burned down, either for real or metaphorically. When grief is coming on strong, make sure to take that time to do something comforting for yourself. Do something that you know will improve your mood. See a comedy. Take up a new musical instrument. Plant some flowers. Order a coffee at a sidewalk café. Walk along a stream, bayou, river, or the sea. Bake some bread. Attend and participate in a community event at the library or elsewhere. Find and visit a local grief group where you're not alone, and you can talk about your loss with others. And keep remembering that grief comes in waves, so we can rest between the waves. So take heart.

An achievement today is_____

_____

_____

_____

_____

_____

JANUARY 6

...Do not fear...

– Luke 5: 10

Another way of looking at mistakes and regrets of the past is to think of the learning experiences we had as a result of any wrong moves on our part. If we learned from our missteps, then this is a good thing. Regrets of the past can be peeled off like the paper thin skins of an onion, revealing the real you, the authentic you underneath all those learning experiences. To learn to be truly our self, and to be true to our self, can take years of living and years of learning what *isn't* our true self. The influence of others and our culture may have obscured our self knowledge. But through trial and error, we learn our true path. And we know this because it feels *right!*

An achievement today is_____

_____

_____

_____

_____

_____

_____

JANUARY 7

...Get up, let us go from here.
— John 14: 31

If we're in a stalled car, or a stuck car, do we just sit there immobile? Or do we call for help? Working our way on, and through, and beyond depression is like getting that stuck car out of the mud, and getting that stalled engine revved up again. But we have to take steps toward doing this. We have to make an all out effort to get the car in gear. It doesn't just happen. But this isn't at all easy to do when we feel such low energy. However, what we can do is to drag our self off that comfy couch and do something that will make us feel better. And it helps to always keep in mind that God helps those who help themselves, and He'll always meet us more than halfway.

An achievement today is_____
_____
_____
_____
_____
_____
_____
_____

JANUARY 8

...For behold, the kingdom of God is in your midst.

– Luke 17: 21

Going through a period of depression gives new meaning to the term, 'self-absorbed.' It's difficult to think about the needs of others because we're so consumed with our own heavy feelings, worries, anxieties, etc. And we tend to be concentrating on worldly matters rather than our spiritual life. It's hard to get out of our own head, our own miseries, and our own distorted view of things. Whether it be our life, or what makes up our environment; if we are feeling depressed, we can bet on the fact that our view is distorted regarding everything we see or hear. There is a saying in 12-Step groups: *Wear the garment of the world loosely.*

An achievement today is_____

_____
_____
_____
_____
_____
_____
_____

JANUARY 9

Now learn the parable from the fig tree: when its branch has already become tender and puts forth its leaves, you know that summer is near.

– Mark 13: 28

A devastating aspect of depression is: the individual believes these despairing feelings are always going to continue. There will be no respite or change. The depressed feelings will go on and on relentlessly. This is one of the greatest misconceptions of the depressed person. The truth is, depressed feelings come and go. There is light at the end of the tunnel, and the tunnel can be short. But, we have to push ourselves, shove ourselves if need be, to fight back against the dense heaviness by doing things that will improve our mood, change our brain chemistry, and lighten the heaviness and inertia and the "stuckness." One sure way to change our inner chemistry is to take a brisk walk, or engage in some other exercise. Then take a moment to notice how this changes our mood and enjoy the glow of it.

An achievement today is_____

_____

_____

_____

JANUARY 10

…because you have been faithful in a very little thing…
— Luke 19: 17

Attending to small details in our daily life can be as important as paying attention to the big things. Measuring twice before cutting or sawing; checking the oil stick in the car; walking the dog; picking up litter tossed to the side of the road; watering the plants; remaining by the stove to stir the pot are all little things, but they can have consequences if they are ignored. (A friend of mine burned his house down by lying down for a "minute" while heating something up on the stove. Another friend burned up her new car engine because she didn't check the oil level before driving off.) Keep in mind that old saying: God is in the details!

An important detail I attended to today_____

_____

_____

_____

_____

_____

_____

_____

JANUARY 11

Behold, I stand at the door and knock; if anyone hears My voice and opens the door, I will come in to him and will dine with him, and he with Me.

– Revelation 3: 20

Open the door? How do I do that? There are many possibilities. By reading Scripture. By listening to teachers of the Word on TV or radio. By visiting churches or synagogues until we find one we want to revisit. By keeping our daily journal up to date and writing down our insights. By praying, any time, any place, out loud or silently. By feeling gratitude and giving thanks for that which we do have, and focusing on that rather than what we want or don't have. And remember the verse: *Draw near to God and He will draw near to you.* James 4: 8

A spiritual insight I had today is:_____

_____

_____

_____

_____

_____

_____

_____

JANUARY 12

*...because you have a little power, and have kept My word
and have not denied My name.*

– Revelation 3: 8

Even if we are experiencing low energy, we can still bring encouragement to another who is suffering and needs some attention. Remember Jesus directs us to visit the sick and those in prison. I have unsung friends who have spent decades quietly visiting inmates and bringing them spiritual concepts and hope. Other friends, one of them a retired doctor, make it a habit to visit people in nursing homes who would otherwise have no visitors. Also, if you read a bit of Jesus' teachings every day, you may have just the right quote to offer someone who is hurting. The right quote at the right time can make a great difference in a friend's life. Jesus' teachings don't have near the impact when closed in a dusty Bible than they do when read and memorized!

Scripture I may memorize is_____

_____

_____

_____

_____

JANUARY 13

Now He is not the God of the dead but of the living; for all live to Him.

– Luke 20: 38

Music lights up the entire brain as is shown in a PET scan. So listening to music is beneficial not only to our spirit, but to our brain function, and our body health. But don't just listen to your favorite music...experiment with other forms. World music is now accessible on You-Tube. We can listen to music from any country or culture by simply researching the music videos on You-Tube. It's exciting to find music that we respond to and love...and perhaps played with instruments we have never heard of... by accessing the riches of the Internet. Researchers have discovered when we listen to music we love, we are releasing the healing chemical Immunoglobulin A into our bodies. So we not only get to enjoy the music, we receive healing also. Listening to music can be a dynamic aid for mood change.

A kind of music I enjoy is_____

_____

_____

_____

_____

JANUARY 14

...but he who humbles himself will be exalted.

– Luke 18: 14

We take our sensory equipment for granted. However, what we hear and smell is so much less of the spectrum than what a dog hears or smells. My outside dogs, even over a hundred feet from the house, can hear me open their dog food bin from behind the closed backdoor. They immediately start barking in anticipation of breakfast. They also can hear someone approaching the house on a bicycle or on foot from at least six hundred feet down the road! Their barking warns me of an approaching stranger long before I would become aware of it. This humbles me, because I realize that whatever we think it is we understand about the mysteries of God and the universe; our perceptions fall far short of the reality.

An achievement today is_____

_____

_____

_____

_____

_____

JANUARY 15

And He who sent Me is with Me; He has not left Me alone,
for I always do the things that are pleasing to Him.

– John 8: 29

Very often the frustration of a handicap can motivate an individual to achieve something they may not otherwise have attempted. A famous thriller writer reports having years of difficulty in school owing to dyslexia. He had to work twice as hard as anyone else just to get through school. Today his stories are so popular that he sells millions of books. But there are many stories of famous people who overcame disabilities. Van Gogh and Dostoyevsky were both temporal lobe epileptics. Mozart was so poor, he was buried in a pauper's grave, and to this day no one has discovered the location of his remains. And Beethoven? Going deaf, yet still composing? How can that be? It's never about the disability. It's about how we perceive the disability.

Something I've had to overcome is_____

_____

_____

_____

_____

_____

JANUARY 16

...the stone which the builders rejected, this become the chief corner stone.

– Luke 20: 17

We can reframe something that troubles us. In other words, look at it in another way. There is a Buddhist saying: *Out of the mud grows the lotus.* Tina Turner repeated that to herself over and over when trying to start a new life after fleeing marital abuse. And negative situations of the past can become the driving force or the fertilizer for a positive and meaningful outcome. There are many organizations that have done monumental works which came out of the despair of their founders. Amber Alert, MADD, A.A., Jessica's Law, are just a few of these. We can turn our despondency, sorrow, or despair into the positive energy needed to achieve our goals. Believe it or not, there is a tremendous storehouse of energy underlying the weight of depressed feelings. We can use that energy and transform it by redirecting it toward something we want to achieve.

Something I can reframe is_____

_____

_____

_____

JANUARY 17

Was the baptism of John from heaven or from men?
— Luke 20: 4

Another way of reframing painful past experiences is this metaphor. Remember the oyster and the pearl. The grain of sand irritates the oyster so much that it creates the pearl. Next time you find yourself reviewing an upsetting past experience or event, remind yourself how the oyster creates the pearl out of discomfort and discord. Probably most of the creative efforts of artists, musicians and writers have been inspired by difficulties. Certainly there have been hundreds of testimonies to this. We can use whatever has disturbed us in the past as fuel for creativity. (Think of all those country music lyrics that turned suffering into hit songs!) When we're creating something, it changes our mood for the better. And we're transforming something hurtful or painful into healing energy whenever we're creating something new.

An achievement today is_____

_____

_____

_____

_____

JANUARY 18

When did we see You sick, or in prison, and come to You?

– Matthew 25: 39

Going through a period of depression can be a lot like being in jail. Locked up…because very often depressed people turn their house into a jail without bars. With curtains drawn and doors locked, they remain inside brooding. This leads to more low energy and despondency, and extends a low mood over even more days or weeks. Just staying indoors shut off from sunshine feeds a dark mood. Light heals! However, awareness is our best tool for rolling back any isolating tendencies. Exercising, studying something to exercise the brain, and practicing coping skills can lighten a heavy mood. A technique called *compartmentalization* can be useful. One way to compartmentalize is to picture a file cabinet in your mind, shut any troubling thoughts into the drawers and slam the drawers shut.

A thought I'd like to shut away is_____
_____
_____
_____
_____
_____

JANUARY 19

...Stretch out your hand!...

– Matthew 12: 13

Depressed people tend to isolate, so they can brood and be left alone to lie about and spin their wheels in the shadows. Yet, it can be so therapeutic to get out of the house and mingle with others. Reaching out can be difficult; however, the effort can bring about a significant change in mood. *If you keep doing what you're doing; you'll keep getting what you're getting.* If you can't think of a friend you care to visit, can you attend a meeting of some support group, go to the library, walk around town, visit a local attraction, attend a local lecture or other event, or register for a course or some lessons? Any break from the preoccupation with self that goes along with depression can be welcome. *Interrupt* the obsessing and circular thinking. And if you can have some laughs, that will really help!

An achievement today is_____

_____

_____

_____

_____

_____

JANUARY 20

*...It is not those who are well who need a physician, but
those who are sick.*

– Luke 5: 31

Practicing yoga isn't just about body positions. It's all
about the breath. When we're depressed, our breathing tends to be shallow. This affects our mood, our
immune system, and our energy level. Practice a few
yoga positions daily, and slowly add more and more
of them, and you will find you're breathing better, deeper, and expanding your lung capacity. The
ancient practice of yoga stresses the breath, and the
more we practice yoga, the more we will remember to
breathe deeply. This helps diminish a depressed mood
in a powerful way. It will even help you sleep soundly.
It's easy to find yoga instruction books and tapes at
the library and used bookstores. There may even be
classes offered in your community. Check it out. You'll
be *really* glad you did!

An achievement today is_____
_____
_____
_____
_____

JANUARY 21

For John the Baptist has come eating no bread and drinking no wine, and you say, 'He has a demon!'

– Luke 7: 33

Do you feel misjudged? Misunderstood? Unfairly treated? Look at the good company you have! John the Baptist himself! Antonia, a Sicilian friend of mine likes to say, "It's none of our business what other people think of us." So true. And if you find you're concerning yourself with what others think of you, repeat this quote often to yourself. Because it's important to remember...it *is* none of our business! That's them! We have our own life to lead... and our own life work to do. And trying to please others won't help us accomplish what we see as our life purpose.

An achievement today is_____

_____

_____

_____

_____

_____

_____

_____

JANUARY 22

The Son of Man has come eating and drinking, and you say, 'Behold, a gluttonous man and a drunkard, a friend of tax collectors and sinners!'

– Luke 7: 34

So much for public opinion! If feelings of rejection or other public opinion have anything to do with a down or dark mood, remember this passage. Also keep in mind what Patsy, a Boston nurse says, "Rejection is God's protection." Think about that. See if Nurse Patsy's comment fits a situation that has bothered or upset you. It may well be you are better off without the person who has hurt you, patronized you, condescended to you, broken off with you, or otherwise rejected you. We can meet new people and maybe make new friends if we get out and about. Why stay stuck and focusing on a person who has hurt us when there are millions of good people out there we haven't even met yet? And if you forgive whoever hurt you…that will free you, *and increase your energy.* Don't give them any more power to sap your energy or your joy!

An achievement today is_____

_____

_____

_____

JANUARY 23

Yet wisdom is vindicated by all her children.

– Luke 7: 35

A daily period of study, whether it be the Bible or other wisdom literature, can be difficult for someone who is depressed. It can be hard to concentrate, and reading comprehension can be spotty. The mind may wander or continue the circular distress thinking despite what is on the page. However, even a few minutes with a good book can be helpful. Just one pertinent sentence can grab our attention and make a big difference in our day, if we stay open to this possibility. Many people throughout the ages and from different cultures and religions have opened their holy book and read just one short passage as a way of beginning the new day.

An achievement today is_____

_____

_____

_____

_____

_____

_____

_____

JANUARY 24

...We played the flute for you, and you did not dance...
– Luke 7: 32

Music is so powerful. We can utilize music therapy every day of our lives. We can learn to manipulate our mood with music and be our own Music Therapist. For example, many people who want to increase their energy to do some heavy work, know they can turn the radio dial to a classic rock station or a classic pop station, and they will feel instantly invigorated. Music is so powerful that musicians actually have measurable brain differences from non-musicians. The Planum Temporale, a part of the cerebral cortex, is larger in the right hemisphere of musicians. *And,* it actually can increase in size when someone who is not a musician takes up an instrument and practices for a long enough period of time.

An instrument I'd like to play is_____

_____

_____

_____

_____

_____

_____

JANUARY 25

Take care what you listen to...

– Mark 4: 24

We know to be careful about nutrition and what we eat. But how many people worry about what they are hearing? There's a lot of "junk food" on TV and radio, yet a lot of people leave TVs and radios on non-stop. There's also a lot of distracting noise in cities and towns. If you have to live in a noisy environment with airplanes, sirens, blaring horns, and loud voices bothering you, consider purchasing ear protectors. I bought a set designed for target practice that protect up to 15 decibels. It can't be too quiet to suit me, so I put these on whenever noise bothers me. Out in the country where I live that could be crop dusters or a neighbor's chain saw or riding mower. Pay attention to your "sound nutrition" as much as your food nutrition. What goes into our ears is just as important as what goes into our mouth.

An achievement today is_____

_____

_____

_____

_____

JANUARY 26

…Your sins have been forgiven you…

– Luke 5: 23

Dr. Bernie Siegel has written so much on how guilt can contribute to illness. Have faith that once we've expressed our remorse over previous actions in prayer, we are forgiven, and can release past mistakes, resolving to learn from them, and knowing we can do better in future. Depressed people are subject to self-recriminations. They can go over and over painful memories of the past. This circular, distress thinking only extends a bout of depression. We can work against this tendency with thought-stopping techniques. One such skill is to say internally, *That was then. This is now!* Another is to visualize a door in your mind and slam it against unwelcome thoughts. Beating ourselves up is not helpful, nor will it lighten a dark mood. Forgive yourself for any unwise or unkind behavior in the past. This is healing. And if you think you should have been perfect all those years, remember: *Most of us are not saints!*

Something I keep guilting myself with is_____
_____
_____
_____

JANUARY 27

...we sang a dirge, and you did not weep.
– Luke 7: 32

Often, when depressed, we may feel the pressure of unshed tears, but be unable to cry. We may wish we could just have a "good cry," but the tears won't come to relieve that heavy feeling. It can be useful to employ some movie therapy, and watch a movie that is likely to have such an effect on us that we will cry. Whether this is because of a happy or a sad ending is immaterial. Crying is therapeutic. Tears wash our eyes, but they wash away much more than that. And, in addition, crying releases good brain chemicals. After a good cry, take note of the big change in how you feel. And don't forget to be mindful of how your breathing changes from shallow breaths to deeper ones after a good cry.

An achievement today is_____

_____

_____

_____

_____

_____

_____

JANUARY 28

…Get up, and pick up your pallet and walk.

– Mark 2: 9

There is a mantra that goes with a depressed mood: *I don't feel like it!* But when feeling the heaviness, stuckness, and the inertia of depression, we *must* move in order to feel better. The longer we can push ourselves to work or exercise, even if we don't feel like it, the more brain chemicals will be released that will improve our mood. Sometimes, an individual can feel so depressed just walking to the mailbox can be an achievement. So give yourself credit and a pat on the back, no matter how much exercise you push yourself to do…and know it will be easier to do even more tomorrow because of what you did today. Prime the pump! (If you have mobility problems, do what you can, whenever you can, as much as you can. And if a physical therapist has outlined certain daily exercises for you, be sure to carry these out.)

An achievement today is_____
_____
_____
_____
_____

JANUARY 29

So the last shall be first, and the first last.
– Matthew 20: 16

Be mindful of how you speak of any depressed mood. Don't own it by saying: *My depression.* Think in terms of a passing mood instead...and don't weigh yourself down with the ownership of depression. Moods are transitional. We may wake up in a lousy mood, but that doesn't mean we have to continue feeling that way all day. We have skills and knowledge of how to transform a bad mood into a good one. We know about how to change inner chemistry through exercise and laughter. We are learning coping skills that effect mood change. We are learning to *interrupt* a bout of negative thinking by getting involved in a project or outside activity that will break that dismal chain of thought. We are noticing the changes within as we practice these coping skills, and we find we are getting better and better at self-coaching our way into improved mood.

A coping skill I practiced today is_____

_____

_____

_____

_____

JANUARY 30

For many are called, but few are chosen.

– Matthew 22: 14

Think it's too late for you to do something you would like? That you're too old to learn a new instrument, or take up dance, or martial arts, or learn a new language? There is research showing that learning a new instrument actually changes our brain...at any age. Even people who have had a stroke can create new pathways in the brain by working at something that is difficult for them. And studying something we want to learn helps keep our brain alert and healthy. And remember, Winston Churchill wrote the multi-volume *History of the English Speaking People* in his eighties. He even had to stand as he wrote, owing to a physical condition that made it painful for him to stay seated. Getting involved in a challenging project helps us shake off murky, self-absorbed thoughts that are sure to lengthen any dismal mood.

An achievement today is_____

_____

_____

_____

_____

JANUARY 31

From the days of John the Baptist until now the kingdom of heaven suffers violence, and violent men take it by force.

– Matthew 11:12

Here Jesus is talking about how the determined will seek and find the kingdom of God. What we seek is what we will find. What we place our focus on is what we will have more of. If we push toward our goal of peace of mind and remain steadfast in our quest, we will approach the kingdom of God that is peace and tranquility. We do this by steady work toward our goal of mental and physical stability. We put into practice that which we know will lead us to a place of peacefulness. Everything Jesus taught us is to help us achieve the goal of daily growing closer to God. Everything he warned us to avoid takes us further in the opposite direction. If we seek an end to fear and anxiety, we cannot focus on fear and anxiety. We keep our eye on the road ahead, not on the road that we have left behind. We remain fully aware of where we are today, and notice the gifts of the day that are all around us. A friend of mine who lost her daughter states her view very firmly in this way: *I never look back!*

Something I did today to seek peace of mind_____

FEBRUARY 1

…You shall not put the Lord your God to the test.

– Luke 4: 12

Here Jesus is responding to the devil with a quote from the 91st Psalm. He frequently quotes from the Old Testament from memory. Having memorized so much of scripture, He has quotes pertinent to the situation instantly at the ready. This is a practice that can be very useful for us in times of need. If we memorize some of our favorite scripture, we will find one of these quotes pop into our mind in a given situation…just when we need it most. It may sound difficult to do, but it really isn't. Try writing down a few of your favorite verses on index cards and keeping them with you until you know them by heart.

A verse that means a lot to me is_____

_____

_____

_____

_____

_____

_____

FEBRUARY 2

...Truly I say to you, no prophet is welcome in his hometown.

– Luke 4: 24

Another example of Jesus alluding to stories of the Old Testament. In this case, he goes on to refer to the story of Elijah and Elisha. The more you learn about the Bible, the more interesting it becomes. It's full of adventures, scandals, wicked actions, murder and more outrageous behavior than you could find in a dozen modern crime novels. Two fascinating books are: *Saints & Scoundrels of the Bible* and *The Harlot By the Side of the Road: Forbidden Tales of the Bible.* These stories are short and easily digested, but reading anything can at times be difficult for a depressed individual as concentration can be affected by a low mood. However, reading exercises and improves brain function, so keep at it.

An achievement today is_____

_____

_____

_____

_____

_____

FEBRUARY 3

...Behold, I say to you, lift up your eyes and look on the fields, that they are white for harvest.

– John 4: 35

We may not think we are ready to feel like ourselves yet. We may think we have to wait a while in order to feel better. However, we can feel better right now! It's always our choice, because a state of mind is *in* the mind! We can *act* as if we're feeling better, even if we don't think we are. Remember that song *One Day at a Time?* Life can seem overwhelming when we're downhearted, but we only have to live *one day at a time.* We can do that! We can stand up straighter and *move.* We can practice various techniques if we're aware of run-on, racing thoughts. One way is to imagine your mind is a room, and you're sweeping it out. Sweeping away any unwelcome, dead-end thoughts until the floor of your mind is clean and uncluttered. Then visualize your mind as a clean, empty room. It's a peaceful image for me. Give it a try.

An achievement today is_____

_____

_____

_____

FEBRUARY 4

Those beside the road are those who have heard; then the devil comes and takes away the word from their heart, so that they will not believe and be saved.

– Luke 8: 12

Have you ever been feeling really good, and then all of a sudden, a worrisome thought enters your mind and brings you down? Whether or not you believe the devil is behind this, you can banish these devilish thoughts! Compartmentalization is a technique taught to the staff in the Clinton White House during the Lewinsky scandal, so they could get work done despite the media storm that raged. One example of compartmentalization is to picture a safe in your mind. Place any unwanted thoughts into the safe. Slam the door shut! Repeat as needed. Coping skills become easier and more effective the more we practice them.

An achievement today is_____

_____

_____

_____

_____

_____

_____

FEBRUARY 5

…if your eye is clear, your whole body will be full of light.
– Matthew 6: 22

No matter what is happening around us, we have the choice of feeling peaceful. We always have the choice of managing our thoughts. If we are disturbed by run-on, painful thoughts, we can always use one of our coping skills to interrupt the noisy unwelcome static in our mind. Another coping skill we may want to practice is to repeat: *I choose peace.* No matter how many times we experience intrusive thoughts today, we can repeat this mantra: *I choose peace.* At the same time we can visualize a pebble slowly dropping to the sandy bottom of a clear, fresh stream. Take note of how this image makes you feel.

A peaceful image for me is_____
_____
_____
_____
_____
_____
_____
_____
_____

FEBRUARY 6

...do not be worried about your life...

– Matthew 6: 25

12-Step groups talk about "pity parties." Sometimes we are feeling so sorry for ourselves that we forget to be grateful for the good things we have. Feeling sorry for ourselves is certain to ensure a continuing lousy mood. However, another 12-Step phrase is: *An attitude of gratitude.* It turns a bad mood around. Gratitude sets up an altogether different inner atmosphere than self-pity. And others near us can feel the "vibes" of our improved mood as well, just by being near to us. We don't even have to say anything. People around us can resonate to our improved mood without our vocalizing it, because we are focusing on our abundance rather than our lack. Studies have shown people often avoid a depressed person. I believe it may be because they don't want that heavy mood to spread to them. They think it might be contagious, like the flu!

Today I am grateful for_____

_____

_____

_____

_____

FEBRUARY 7

Blessed are those who mourn, for they shall be comforted.

– Matthew 5: 4

Could part of your low mood be due to the anniversary of a painful event? A loved one's death? Sometimes people aren't even aware of this affecting their peace of mind. If this is the case, be sure to plan fun activities for yourself in days leading up to and around the anniversary. See that you arrange some treats for yourself. Be kind to yourself. And really work your support system. Go to any support groups you care to. Contact friends and socialize. Take in a movie. And be sure to exercise. Take a brisk walk. Listen to favorite music. Do something nice for someone else to take your mind off yourself. It's been reported that a great majority of hospital stays, for any reason, have a root cause of unresolved grief…(accidents included).

An achievement today is_____
_____
_____
_____
_____
_____

FEBRUARY 8

So do not worry about tomorrow; for tomorrow will take care of itself...

– Matthew 6: 34

Marilyn, a highly effective nurse-manager of the psychiatric hospital where I worked, often tells depressed clients: "You have one foot in yesterday, and the other in tomorrow, and you're p***ing on today!" Each time we find ourselves brooding about the past or future, we can remember Marilyn's quote, and focus on today. We can remind ourselves to really look at what we're seeing as we go through the day. Am I so caught up in worry thoughts that I'm missing life bursting out all around me...the songbird singing its little heart out, the chattering squirrel, the cloud formation tinged with gold, the tiny violets? Am I throwing away today because of living in the shadowy past or future. Keep in mind the 12-Step saying: *The present is really a present!*

Something I enjoyed seeing today is_____

_____

_____

_____

_____

_____

FEBRUARY 9

...to the extent that you did it to one of these brothers of Mine, even the least of them, you did it to Me.

– Matthew 25: 40

No matter how small an act of kindness we perform, our spiritual growth advances. Whenever we give our time and energy to help another, we are truly following Jesus' guidance for our lives. (And that includes helping ourselves, because we deserve kindness as well.) If experiencing a down mood, we may be blinded to the needs of others...and our own self. We may ignore or overlook possibilities for kindness. And this also includes animals and plants. Conversely, every time that we do something to help another live better, we will feel improved mood. For example, I have a friend who struggles with chronic pain from an old accident. Yet Lenore makes the time to read stories to the blind over the radio on a regular basis.. She gets much pleasure from this, and reports a marked decrease in the pain on those scheduled broadcasting days.

An achievement today is_____

_____

_____

_____

FEBRUARY 10

...first clean the inside of the cup and of the dish, so that the outside of it may become clean also.

– Matthew 23: 26

Did you know the qualities we find so irritating in others are the very qualities we ourselves possess? It's much easier to see them in others than to recognize them in our self. We may not even be aware we have these annoying characteristics as part of our personality because we've suppressed them. We call this our *shadow self.* And a sure way of discovering what our shadow self is made up of is to notice what annoys us most in others! These hidden personality traits that we keep under wraps and under the radar are better acknowledged than denied. When we acknowledge our shadow self, we may find we are more tolerant of others' behavior and less judgmental. This frees us to become more authentic, more real, and allows us to experience more energy as well. Suppressing anything takes up a lot of energy!

An achievement today is_____

_____

_____

_____

FEBRUARY 11

For everyone who asks receives, and he who seeks finds, and to him who knocks it will be opened.

– Matthew 7: 8

For socialization, we can read the local newspaper's community calendar. Support groups are often listed for all sorts of physical problems and addictions. There are groups for overeaters, gambling addiction, smokers, and of course alcoholism and drug addiction. There are even groups for sex addicts! If you're in a small town and can't find a local group to suit your particular needs, you may want to research available groups in a larger, nearby town. There are also grief groups for special circumstances such as the loss of a child. There are support groups for codependents, caretakers, families of the mentally ill, poor anger management, for those with emotional distress (Emotions Anonymous), and recovering heart patients. Another way of finding groups that are available nearby is through the library or United Way or churches and synagogues.

An achievement today is_____

_____

_____

_____

FEBRUARY 12

...I showed you many good works from the Father...
– John 10: 32

There is an old Hasidic story that when a person dies, God asks them if they used the talents they were born with during their lifetime. If their answer is no, and they give excuses why not, their answer is dismissed. Today honor the gifts and talents you were given by utilizing them in some way. Whatever your talent is, use it, practice it, express it, create something with it. Sing, dance, draw, make something with your hands, paint, or work with animals or plants. Please don't say you weren't given any gifts or talents, because *everybody* has unique gifts! As you practice your talents, your expertise will advance quickly, and your capabilities will be strengthened. This shows respect for our gifts and gratitude for them. Just because you haven't been using your talents, doesn't mean you can't start again now. And don't tolerate that lament that goes along with depression: "I don't feel like it!" or "I don't have time". If you can watch TV each day or evening, then you *do* have the time.

A talent I haven't been using is_____

_____

_____

_____

FEBRUARY 13

I am the door; if anyone enters through Me, he will be saved, and will go in and out and find pasture.

–John 10: 9

Sometimes if feeling depressed, we can feel so alone and even abandoned. Even feeling lonely when around people. A lot of this has to do with preoccupation with our own obsessive thoughts. At times like this it is helpful to remember God is omnipresent. If God is everywhere, He is right there with you at this moment, surrounding you with light. You are not alone, but depression distorts thought, and leads to misguided perceptions. Today feel gratitude for grace. Grace is a gift, and because of grace, we have faith and believe in a Higher Power. Be aware of being surrounded by God's light like a cloud of protection. Feeling all alone is a delusion and a harmful side effect of depression.

An achievement today is_____

_____

_____

_____

_____

_____

FEBRUARY 14

…Blessed are you who are poor, for yours is the kingdom of God.

– Luke 6: 20

During Mardi Gras season in Louisiana, (and other states, especially Alabama, where it all started in our country,) it's easy to find fun things to do. There are many opportunities including parades, costumes, King cakes, parties, and live music. We may feel we are at the bottom of the emotional barrel. Our stomach may feel tight, our head splitting, and our heart pierced, but we can *interrupt* all that and get out there and participate in the celebration. That's what we do for small children when they're upset or crying. We turn their attention to something new. We engage their interest in something else to get their mind off whatever was upsetting them. It also works with adults…even our own self.

An achievement today is_____

_____

_____

_____

_____

_____

FEBRUARY 15

Be glad in that day and leap for joy...
– Luke 6: 23

Today pretend you're happy, even if you aren't. Do something you would do if you were feeling like your old self. Something pleasing to you. Remember our inner child has probably been neglected if we have been feeling downcast. Our inner child wants to have some fun, and we will reap the benefits of arranging for some fun by feeling more energy and better health. Ask your inner child for a suggestion as to what he/she would like to do today. The answer will pop into your head right away or soon after. My family has three paraplegic friends who laugh and pursue activities almost every day. They get out and about, socialize, and do more than some people I know who have the full use of their arms and legs. We can show *an attitude of gratitude* for our mobility by using our arms and legs and exercising daily.

Something my inner child wants to do is_____

_____

_____

_____

_____

FEBRUARY 16

But seek first His kingdom and His righteousness, and all these things will be added to you.

– Matthew 6: 33

You know it is said that God provides us with everything we need. Often though, we think we know what we need, and we aren't getting it, so we feel deprived and frustrated. An "I want this, and I want that," sort of mantra. One of the ways we can work our way out of this trap of desiring that which we don't need is to make a list of everything for which we feel grateful. This can result in a feeling of abundance, rather than a sense of lack. Always remember the old saying, "He who knows he has enough is rich." Repeat the affirmation: *Everything I need comes to me,* whenever you find yourself wanting still something else you don't have and probably don't need. Remember we've been brainwashed and manipulated by advertising for all of our lives...and all the advertisers want is our money. No kidding!

Something I want, but don't need is_____

_____

_____

_____

_____

FEBRUARY 17

but I have prayed for you, that your faith may not fail...
– Luke 22: 32

You know the old saying, "You have to break eggs to make an omelet." Many times we have had to lose something in order to make way for something new... and something still better. The other old saying, "One door closes and then the other door opens," is also true. We have to let go of something that is no longer what we need, in order to make room for what is needed for our new way of being, our new adventure, and our new growth. Today you can exercise your faith by reminding yourself that something new is emerging out of any dark mood. That you are emerging from any losses, and that you will reach a new plateau as you step up and beyond where you are now. Remind yourself that this is a transitional period, and you will feel even more fully alive and actualized after shedding this low mood.

Something I can let go of today is_____
_____
_____
_____
_____

FEBRUARY 18

...when the Son of Man comes, will He find faith on the earth?

– Luke 18: 8

There is such a noticeable difference in plants after a good rain. Any gardener or farmer will tell you that rainwater does wonders that no amount of watering with tap water will do. There are so many mysteries in nature that science has yet to explain. And there are many mysteries in faith that the unbeliever cannot fathom. As we exercise our faith, we find ourselves healing and becoming whole with more and more periods of peace of mind and serenity. Like plants growing faster with the rain, we respond rapidly when we allow God's love to grow within us. Today I will silence any disturbing thoughts that drown out spiritual guidance. I can't hear spiritual direction if my mind is filled with static. Mother Theresa said that when she prays she doesn't talk, she *listens!*

Guidance I heard today is_____

_____

_____

_____

_____

FEBRUARY 19

For where your treasure is, there your heart will be also.

– Luke 12: 34

We can do things symbolically to improve mood. In a private place we can put something that represents our healing. Anything that expresses our sense of the sacred. Maybe a candle, a feather we found, a special stone, or flower. Or it can simply be a chair that we use repeatedly for our meditative, prayerful time. Perhaps instead of an arranged place, you prefer a natural setting such as the beach, a stream, the woods, or a park. A preacher I know leaves his family early in the morning and drives to the same spot where he reads his Bible and prays while sitting in his car. Wherever you choose for your contemplative time, make it where you won't be disturbed and where it's quiet. This will serve as an anchoring place for new insights that will help your situation.

A Jewish saying is: *Wherever you pray, there is your temple.*

A private place I like to go is_____

_____

_____

_____

_____

FEBRUARY 20

Now suppose one of you fathers is asked by his son
for a fish; he will not give him a snake instead of a
fish, will he?
– Luke 11: 11

Have you honored your inner child yet by doing what
he/she asked to do for fun? If it's a reasonable request
from our inner child, we need to arrange to do it. The
benefits for doing so will increase our creativity, our
immunity, our energy, and improve our mood. This
is a lot of positive feedback for what is probably a very
simple request for something fun to do. When we
please our inner child, even the colors around us will
seem brighter, and certainly our eyes and smile will be
brighter also. When we ask depressed people in the
psychiatric unit what they've done for fun lately, they
almost invariably say: Nothing! This is a sure formula
for a sustained lousy mood.

Something I did for my inner child today is_____
_____
_____
_____
_____

FEBRUARY 21

For many are called, but few are chosen.

– Matthew 22: 14

Being alone is what some people desire, as they prefer their own company. Being alone is also what some other people will do almost anything to avoid. Life is so much easier if you can develop a real appreciation for being alone. Where you can pursue your interests, be a self starter and work on your projects without interruption. However, many people would actually rather be with someone they don't much like in order not to be alone. And there's a big difference between feeling lonely and enjoying solitude. But, when experiencing a depressed mood, getting out and about can interrupt the stale "stuckness". Often depression is a signal that a person is at a crossroads and isn't sure of their next move. Events may have brought them to a turning point and possibly a whole new way of life, once they make up their mind in which direction to go. Contemplating your next move is smart, but if it turns into a doom and gloom session, then a change of scenery is in order.

A new direction I may take is_____

_____

_____

_____

FEBRUARY 22

or a bag for your journey, or even two coats, or sandals, or a staff...

– Matthew 10: 10

Self-comforting comes in many forms. What are some of the ways you can comfort yourself when you're feeling low? Sometimes people self-comfort in ways that are harmful. They may go shopping and run up debt, causing pain later. Some self-comfort with food that puts on unwanted weight, which makes them feel badly later. Some abuse cigarettes, alcohol, or drugs, or develop a gambling addiction. But there are also positive addictions. We can become addicted to activities such as jogging, walking, dancing, martial arts, practicing music, etc. We can experience the bliss of natural mind/body chemicals which are released by positive addictions. And we can experience withdrawal symptoms when we don't do these things, just as the alcoholic or addict does when they quit their drug of choice.

A positive addiction I have is_____
_____
_____
_____

FEBRUARY 23

If you then, being evil, know how to give good gifts to your children, how much more will your Father who is in heaven give what is good to those who ask Him!

– Matthew 7: 11

One of the errors in thinking that a bout of depression can cause is that we are overwhelmed and helpless. To take charge of another gloomy day seems futile. Yet the "parent" part of us can take over and direct the plans for the day, even though the low energy part of us doesn't "feel like doing anything." The parent part of us can push us into action. We may think we're so behind why bother even trying, what's the use? But, remembering to break the job down into increments is a very effective way of catching up fast. Once we do a little, we are energized, and find ourselves doing even more, and then more the next day and the next. God is in the details, and every small portion we get done builds momentum and gives us hope we will get the job done after all. *The secret is to get started..even just a little bit!*

A job I can do by increments is_____

_____

_____

_____

FEBRUARY 24

I have come as Light into the world, so that everyone who believes in Me will not remain in darkness.

– John 12: 46

If in a dark mood, we may hide from the light, but it's imperative that we get outside and absorb all the light we can, even if the days are overcast. We still get some benefit from sunlight on gray or cloudy days, and we need to do this if we want to elevate our mood. We can't afford to do anything that we know will only add to the gloom of a dark mood. A friend of mine takes this to heart. She can't bear to be indoors, and takes everything she can outside to do it, including her sewing! She just sets up a worktable in the backyard. Back when we were children, they couldn't even get us to come inside for supper. Remember those days? When we were so enthralled with whatever we were doing we even forgot when it was time to eat!

Something I can do outside is_____

_____

_____

_____

_____

_____

FEBRUARY 25

...What did you go out into the wilderness to see? A reed shaken by the wind?

– Matthew 11:7

Remember that one of depression's pitfalls is to think these heavy feelings are going to go on endlessly. Weather changes. The wind shifts all the time, and so do our moods. There's an old saying that a day that starts out with everything going wrong is a day that will turn out to be great! So stay free of any ideas that the way you feel when you wake up in the morning is the way you're going to feel all day. Look for and expect good things to happen. I have a hard time in the morning, so often I ask God to send me a surprise gift. Then I go outside with my coffee and start looking for it with anticipation because I *expect* to find it. This is how I reframe my mornings, and you can too if you wish.

A good thing today is_____

_____

_____

_____

_____

_____

_____

FEBRUARY 26

Enter through the narrow gate...
– Matthew 7: 13

It is said that whatever we focus on in life is what we are going to get in life. If we only focus on the negative, we'll get more of the same. By focusing on what we're trying to achieve, however, rather than what we don't want, we're moving steadily toward our goals. If going through a down mood, we have a tendency to see only that which annoys or irritates us. We can counteract this, by purposely looking for what is pleasing. And don't forget to look up, rather than down. Up will reveal beautiful cloud formations, sunrises, sunsets, the different shapes of trees, squirrel nests, birds, and the stars. All this beauty will take our minds off that tedious preoccupation with self which is the hallmark of depression.

Something I saw when looking up today is_____

_____

_____

_____

_____

_____

_____

FEBRUARY 27

But the one who endures to the end, he will be saved.

– Matthew 24: 13

Persistence! Don't be disheartened if up against a frustrating situation. Persist in what you know is right. Stand up for yourself. And do it over and over if necessary. Once when dealing with Customer Service regarding weeks of terrible service on my cell phone, I received no assistance, only the brush off. However, after nagging them over and over, they finally gave me the "Escalation Department" number. Once I called there, I received immediate satisfaction. Be persistent, but at the same time remember you get more flies with honey than vinegar. Be firm, but polite, when trying to sort out a frustrating problem. And if working to resolve a problem with a corporation, always keep a notebook of dates, times you called, and the name of the person you spoke to.

Corporations fear my friends Barbara and Lenore, because they don't give up, are persistent, and *always* keep a log of their phone calls.

An achievement today is_____

_____

_____

_____

FEBRUARY 28

...for you do not know the day nor the hour.

– Matthew 25: 13

We can feel so impatient, forgetting to enjoy the process of doing a job...just wanting to get it over with. We want instant success. God's time often seems to take so long! We need to remember that our sense of time is man made, contrived, and quite different from God's time. Remember our sense of time as children? Waiting for something just a day or two seemed endless. The older we get the faster time goes. So our sense of time is constantly changing. If we're having fun, time whips by. If we're bored, we keep watching the clock. If, however, we learn to take pleasure in the *process* of doing something, then we can actually enjoy the work.

An achievement today is_____

_____

_____

_____

_____

_____

_____

_____

FEBRUARY 29

...Sit at My right hand...
– Matthew 22: 44

Resting in the moment often during the day and evening can be so refreshing. You've noticed cats staring off into space for long periods during the day? Dogs lounge, cross their paws, and stare off as well. Learn from the animals and take frequent rest breaks by allowing yourself to stare out the window and daydream. It is helpful to the immune system and it replenishes energy. Then we can return to whatever task we're occupied with and notice increased motivation and alertness. We may even have picked up some creative ideas during the time-out, daydreaming session. Sitting there and brooding, however, doesn't count as creative daydreaming!

An achievement today is_____

_____

_____

_____

_____

_____

_____

MARCH 1

...go to the sea and throw in a hook, and take the first fish that comes up...

– Matthew 17: 27

At the psychiatric hospital, we heard the same words over and over from depressed clients: "I love to go fishing (or camping, or fill in the blank,) more than anything, but I haven't done any of it for years." Often a bout of depression can be a rebellion by that part of us that wants to enjoy life and have fun. But, by squelching and neglecting that part of us, we set ourselves up for a mood nose-dive. By paying attention and listening to that part of us, however, we can honor that need and pursue an activity that will raise our spirits. But not just as an isolated experience. Recreational activity needs to be included in our lives on a regular basis. And lying on the couch and watching TV does not qualify!

Something I've not done for a while is_____

_____

_____

_____

_____

_____

_____

MARCH 2

*...did you not sow good seed in your field? How then does it
have tares?*

– Matthew 13: 27

Remember weeding your garden after a heavy rain-
storm? Did the weeds shoot up overnight like Jack's
beanstalk? Even if there were no weeds before the
rains, they can pop up by the dozens. If we've had a
heavy rain in our life, painful thoughts can pop up just
like weeds in the garden. It's easier to weed when there
are just a few stragglers, but after a heavy rain, when
they are everywhere, it's much more difficult. If we've
just endured a storm in our life, we may find weeding
out hurtful thoughts a real challenge.

Take courage! It can be done. Imagine a thick mist
swirling around and obscuring any painful thoughts
from the past. Then watch as that image from the
unhappy event is enfolded in mist and disappears
from view.

An achievement today is_____

_____

_____

_____

_____

MARCH 3

Salt is good; but if the salt becomes unsalty, with what will you make it salty again?...

– Mark 9: 50

When I was growing up, pressure cookers were frequently used. I was taught to be extremely careful when cooking with one. Leaving a pressure cooker unattended was not ever to be done. If the cook grew careless around a pressure cooker, severe burns and hospitalization might be the result. So it is with our feelings. If we have been collecting stream within from unresolved anger and resentments, we can blow up just like the unwatched cooker. It's important to express volatile feelings in a safe manner. Safety valves may include a punching bag, exercise, a therapeutic yell, and talking about it with a professional or friend. Writing and art therapy work wonders also. Sherri, a talented art therapist friend, stresses to her groups: *When you express the feeling by putting it down on paper, this changes it!* Converting feelings into creative effort is a special kind of alchemy. And it *can* be done.

An achievement today is_____

_____

_____

_____

MARCH 4

*The good man brings out of his good treasure what is good;
and the evil man brings out of his evil treasure what is evil.*

– Matthew 12: 35

Billy Joel suffered a huge betrayal by a trusted friend. Shocked and depressed by this, all he knew to do was to get up in the morning, go to the piano and compose and play music. He worked his way through the trauma this way, and ended up with a whole new album of music. He had transformed the resentment, disbelief, and anger into music and song. Alchemy! Wherever our talents lie, we can transform whatever we're going through into something new and fresh. Much of the world's most beloved stories and artistic endeavor is the result of transforming the energy of pain and tough times into the energy to create. Rumpelstiltskin bragged, "I can turn straw into gold!" We can too.

An achievement today is_____

_____

_____

_____

_____

_____

MARCH 5

...If anyone wants to be first, he shall be last of all and servant of all.

– Mark 9: 35

Moran Samuel, an Israeli woman, woke up paralyzed from the chest down at age 24 owing to a rare stroke in the spine. She worked to become a top performer in wheelchair basketball, and then began rowing competitively. Moran Samuel went on to won a gold medal in an International rowing competition in Italy! Individuals like this can inspire us to push on harder and longer, instead of that tired old, "I don't feel like it. Maybe tomorrow." And then there's my friend's spunky little dog, who lost her leg to a car accident, but gets around like Roadrunner on three legs! Once again, it's not the disability that is the problem...it's the attitude we have toward the disability.

Someone who has inspired me is_____

_____

_____

_____

_____

_____

_____

MARCH 6

even as You gave Him authority over all flesh....
– John 17: 2

Jesus well understands the natural man. That worldly part of us that wants more and more and is never satisfied. That worldly part that holds grudges, seeks vengeance, envies others, etc. Jesus knows all about our worldly self, and teaches us in order to free us. If we are able to follow his guidance we can be free of the weight of resentments and anger towards others. When we are free to bask in the joy of the kingdom, then we are truly blessed. Sometimes this can be the task of a lifetime. To get there, we need daily reminders of His lessons to us. If we can't quite bring ourselves to forgive someone, then we can ask in prayer for help with this. For as many times as we need to, over and over if necessary. It's not for *them* that we want to forgive, but to lighten up that tiresome, heavy baggage we've been hauling around. *Forgiveness heals!*

An achievement today is _____

_____

_____

_____

_____

MARCH 7

For nothing is hidden, except to be revealed....
– Mark 4: 22

Dream images can be so interesting. When we dream of a house, we are most likely dreaming of our self. Is the house grand or small, dark or light, cluttered or empty, sprawling or cramped? Water usually represents our subconscious. Is the water calm or stormy? Are we in a boat or on shore? To find out more about these universal dream images, seek out a high quality dream interpretation book. If we take the time to write down what we remember of our dreams, we will understand more and more what our dreams are telling us. For those who can't remember their dreams, just writing down any small detail and dating it, will help the recall of more and more in subsequent days. Talking about dreams with a friend can be helpful as well.

An achievement today is_____

_____

_____

_____

_____

_____

_____

MARCH 8

...Observe how the lilies of the field grow; they do not toil nor do they spin.

– Matthew 6: 28

The old cliché, "The best things in life are free," is well known. Larry King interviewed Dick Clark, and he talked about how he enjoyed the simplest pleasures more than anything else in life. He said he'd made a great deal of money during his career, and could afford to do whatever he wanted, yet he mostly liked to do the simplest things such as taking walks, picnics, fishing, etc. Even if we're broke, there are hundreds of things we can do to have fun and enjoy life. Things that are often overlooked by people in our consumer oriented, fast track culture. As for me, just give me a country road and a dog or two to walk, and I'm going to be happy. And that hasn't changed since I was very young, so I know this pleases my inner child...always a good way to lighten up quickly.

Something simple I like to do is_____

_____

_____

_____

_____

MARCH 9

...For the mouth speaks out of that which fills the heart.
– Matthew 12: 34

Sometimes when a person is chronically dissatisfied with their life and disappointed in the way things turned out for them, they may take pleasure in another's misfortune or failure. The German word for this is: *Schadenfreude.* Conversely, when we're feeling great and loving life, we wish everyone well, and it's easy to love even difficult people. So, if you've been feeling a bit down lately, and have noticed a twinge of *Schadenfreude*, remember that our thinking is influenced by our moods, just as our moods are greatly influenced by our thinking. Today I will take note of any unkind thoughts about others, and remind myself that as my mood lightens up, those unkind thoughts will dissipate just as the sun burns off the morning fog.

An achievement today is_____

_____

_____

_____

_____

_____

_____

MARCH 10

...Are you still sleeping and resting?...
– Matthew 26: 45

Did you know that your mind has what is called a "basin of attraction?" This means everything and anything that we do towards achieving a goal, no matter how small a step, increases the capacity of the basin of attraction. Each step taken makes working toward that goal easier and easier owing to the deepening of the basin of attraction in our mind. If today I take a step toward achieving a short term or a long term goal, this shows I'm advancing and making progress toward it. This step may just be reading an article about it, or cutting out a picture pertaining to it and hanging it up on the wall, where I can be reminded of it often.

A short term goal I have is_____

_____

_____

_____

_____

_____

_____

_____

MARCH 11

You will be hearing of wars and rumors of wars. See that you are not frightened…

– Matthew 24: 6

You've heard of fasting from food. Have you heard of fasting from TV news? A good friend of mine refuses to watch the news…ever! She says if there's something she needs to know, a friend will alert her to it. The reason she gives for not watching the news is: "Hearing the news makes me feel angry so often because there's so much wrong in the world, so I don't watch because I don't like feeling angry." If you find, like my friend, that you don't like the way you feel after watching the news, take a break from it. (The news today reports a study that finds sitting and watching three hours of TV or movies a day is hard on the heart!) Uh-oh! Even more reason to get up and get moving instead.

An achievement today is_____
_____
_____
_____
_____
_____
_____

MARCH 12

…Get up and come forward!….
– Luke 6: 8

Those friends I have mentioned who are paraplegic were very popular and also highly active before their accidents. One of them ran the sound for a New York rock band; however, a scaffolding broke while he was helping a friend paint his house. The other was an athlete, but was hurt in a car crash the night of his eighteenth birthday. Despite these tragic events, both men have a great sense of humor, remain active in their wheelchairs, and still socialize often. They live full lives, despite the damage, and their attitude is inspirational. It's never about the disability; it's about the way the individual perceives the disability. Some of us with full use of our bodies might as well be in a wheelchair, because we are so sedentary, and don't move!

The kind of exercise I did today is_____

_____

_____

_____

_____

_____

MARCH 13

...blessed are those who hear the word of God and observe it.

– Luke 11: 28

Feeling bored? Sometimes boredom can be an excellent path to reach the serenity of the kingdom. A steady diet of excitement, stimulation, distractions, amusements, and real life drama can create a stream of adrenaline that becomes addictive. A routine, everyday quiet, small town sort of life can be dull and boring to someone addicted to a big city pace. But such a slower paced "dull" life can be a faster path to peace and serenity. And peace and serenity is what the kingdom is all about. If there's nothing much going on in your life and you are bored, reframe it: This is good! I have more opportunity to study, learn new things, notice the wonders all around me, and listen to my inner guidance without all the distractions.

An achievement today is_____

_____

_____

_____

_____

_____

MARCH 14

... you of little faith, why did you doubt?
– Matthew 14: 31

One night, driving home to Florida from a vacation house, I was unable to keep going because of severe thunderstorms, and couldn't see to drive. It was night-time but I couldn't check into a motel because I had my cats and dogs in the back of the pickup. I pulled off the highway and tried to come up with a plan. All I could think to do was to park in the well-lighted parking lot of an Arby's there in Alabama for the night. The staff told me I was welcome to do that, but there was a motel nearby they thought might take me in even with the animals. I went to the motel and even though they had a no-pet policy, the night clerk let me stay there and bring the cages into the room out of the cold rain. Today I will exercise my faith by remembering that God sends us what we need, and often when we least expect it. God *really* does work in mysterious ways.

A saving experience I've had is_____
_____
_____
_____
_____

MARCH 15

The wind blows where it wishes and you hear the sound of it,
but do not know where it comes from and where it is going;
so is everyone who is born of the Spirit.

– John 3: 8

When the March wind blows, picture it blowing away all hurt from the past. Allow its cleansing properties to blow away any unwelcome thoughts from your mind. Allow it to blow through your body also, clearing out all toxins, and anything that could interfere with your perfect health and good energy level. Even a slight breeze can clear the air, but a windy day can clear the air and also our mind of much that is unwanted. Using metaphors such as this can be a powerful tool for elevating our mood. Relish the wind.
Luxuriate in the breezes.

An achievement today is_____
_____
_____
_____
_____
_____
_____
_____

MARCH 16

…and nothing will be impossible to you.

– Matthew 17: 20

Are you a perfectionist? Did you know perfectionists have a harder time getting the job done than those of us who aren't? Perfectionists often work from a place of fear. Fear that their work won't be perfect. Consequently they fiddle with it and delay getting the job done, going over and over it until it's exactly right. They can even delay completing the job altogether because of these internal demands. Frequently perfectionist behavior results in depression because of all the undone projects in their life. Are you putting off starting something because of unrealistic and impractical demands? Because your inner "overseer" is so strict, that it's easier to not do it at all?

I'm a perfectionist about_____

_____

_____

_____

_____

_____

_____

MARCH 17

....blessed are your eyes, because they see...
– Matthew 13: 16

I met a lovely woman from Germany who lived in an upscale resort on the Gulf Coast. She kept a beautiful flower garden in front of the motel she and her husband owned. She had been diagnosed with cancer and working in the garden helped her feel better. The neighborhood "association" complained that some of her flowering plants were "weeds" and demanded she pull them out. My friend felt hurt and confused by this as all the flowering plants in her garden had beautiful blooms. So often people can't see reality because they confuse it with labels. Today I will look for beauty wherever I find it. If it's a wildflower or a weed in a ditch, I will notice it. If it's a "homely" or "unattractive" person, I will look past exteriors to their shining soul.

Something "homely" that I find beautiful is_____

_____

_____

_____

_____

_____

_____

MARCH 18

Nevertheless do not rejoice in this, that the spirits are subject to you, but rejoice that your names are recorded in heaven.

– Luke 10: 20

Affirmations are powerful techniques for changing our perspective. Say them aloud and with conviction. They help to reprogram the mind. Some examples: I *am* a child of God. I *am* protected. I *am* being guided. I *am* healing. I *am* feeling stronger every day. I *am* feeling more alive. We need to counter balance those *non*firmations that rattle around in our head when depressed. I'm so tired. I can't do this. I'm so miserable, etc. Use affirmations as often as you remember to do so, and continue to monitor your thoughts, plucking out those weeds!

An affirmation I like is_____

_____

_____

_____

_____

_____

_____

_____

MARCH 19

Ask, and it will be given to you; seek, and you will find;
knock, and it will be opened to you.

– Matthew 7: 7

Two famous and beautiful songs were written out of intense grief. *Here Come Those Tears Again* which Jackson Browne sings, was written by a mother grieving the loss of her daughter. *Tears in Heaven* was written by Eric Clapton after the tragic death of his little boy. Millions of people have heard and loved those two songs. These are more examples of the alchemy that occurs when we transform our feelings into creativity. There are many, many other songs written from a place of grief. And poetry, paintings, sculptures, and novels as well. Experiment with transforming feelings into some form of creative effort today.

Something I can create is_____

_____

_____

_____

_____

_____

_____

_____

MARCH 20

... The things that are impossible with people are possible with God.

– Luke 18: 27

The second Law of Thermodynamics says that everything tends to entropy. In other words, it's natural for things to break up, fall apart, disorganize, run down, and wear out. So what's new? If you've been feeling depressed lately, you may have low tolerance for this natural state of affairs. It's always something! The toaster's only toasting on one side. The back tire needs air. The hinges squeak on the back door. You lost a favorite earring. The faucet needs a new washer. On and on it goes, day after day. If frustrated with still another glitch in your day, comfort yourself with knowing this is the natural way of things in the universe, and when we're feeling good, these things won't bother us nearly as much as when our energy is low. It may help to repeat that quote: *God is greater than any problem we may have.*

An achievement today is_____
_____
_____
_____
_____

MARCH 21

The one who listens to you listens to Me, and the one who rejects you rejects Me; and he who rejects Me rejects the One who sent Me.

– Luke 10: 16

Sometimes we experience a depressed mood because others are not doing what we'd like. We may have been shocked or dismayed by another's actions. We may have been betrayed by a trusted friend. It's helpful to remember we have no control over others. *Persons, Places, and Things* is repeated often in 12-step groups. This is to help us remember we only have control over our own response to persons, places, and things. Managing our own response and our own serenity is what we are called to do. We learn to rely only on ourselves and our Higher Power. We learn that strengthening that connection is the business we need to attend to first, and all else will follow.

Persons, places or things that I've let disturb me are__

_____

_____

_____

_____

_____

MARCH 22

Are not five sparrows sold for two cents? Yet not one of them is forgotten before God.

– Luke 12: 6

Everybody is doing the best they can, is a way to look at those who are all around us, and ourselves as well. Some are slow moving and have low energy owing to emotional or physical pain. Some have overcome their handicaps or addictions, or past traumas, disappointments and regrets, and are feeling great and pushing forward with hope and energy. Some are going through a downward spiral, while others are on the move, and some seem to stay always at a level peaceful place. Some appear well off financially, yet remain stuck in an unproductive or unhappy phase. Some have low income, yet are content and cheerful and enjoy their life. There's no telling, really, about how others are managing their emotional state or their lives. The only person whose life we can manage is our own. When we judge others for the way they behave, we're being short-sighted, because we don't know all that they are dealing with. Only God knows the whole story. And we need only attend to our own path. Something I attended to today is_____

_____

_____

MARCH 23

...A man planted a vineyard...
– Luke 20: 9

Digging therapy? What's that? Well, if I'm going through a stressful or difficult situation, I turn to digging therapy. I find digging with a shovel in the dirt redirects my thoughts, wears down the restlessness that can accompany anxiety, changes my brain chemistry, and keeps me fit besides. Maybe you'd like to dig a garden to prepare the beds for spring. Maybe you'd like to dig up some grass to make room for a garden. Digging is great exercise, and really helps change depressed feelings into a much more comfortable inner space. If you live in an apartment and have no yard, maybe there's a community garden project nearby you can join. Or maybe you know someone who would love to have you do the digging for their garden. If you're not into digging therapy, try buying some potting soil and repotting nursery plants. You'll feel great when you see all those potted plants lined up.

An achievement today is_____

_____

_____

_____

MARCH 24

... In the world you have tribulation, but take courage; I have overcome the world.

–John 16: 33

A part of our personality that may be suppressed when we are going through a low period, is the part that likes to look great, be stylish, and perhaps receive some admiring glances when out and about. Too often, when feeling lowdown, we may prefer to wear drab colors or black and yank any old thing out of the closet. If we honor that part of us that wants to look our best, we may choose brighter colors and take some time fixing ourselves up before going out into the world. We don't have to choose bright colors necessarily, but colors that bring out our eyes and cast a glow over our skin are going to make us feel lighter and kick our confidence meter up a notch or two.

Colors I choose today are_____

_____

_____

_____

_____

_____

_____

MARCH 25

...and your heart will rejoice, and no one will take your joy away from you.

–John 16: 22

There are many parts to our personality. Some parts get neglected, suppressed, or otherwise ignored. One part of our personality that we would do well to pay attention to is our healthy part; that aspect of our personality that wants us to live in as healthy a manner as possible. When we are engaging in unhealthy, perhaps addictive behaviors, we conveniently suppress our healthy part. Today I want to give the healthy part of my personality a chance to take the lead and program my day. If I do this, the energy I receive in return will be a welcome bonus, and we'll feel great because of it.

Today my healthy part wants _____

_____

_____

_____

_____

_____

_____

_____

MARCH 26

…What is the kingdom of God like, and to what shall I compare it? It is like a mustard seed, which a man took and threw into his own garden…

– Luke 13: 18, 19

Carrying symbols of Scripture can be helpful reminders of favorite passages. I received a bracelet for a gift when I was a child. I have never forgotten it, because it had a small translucent globe with a mustard seed embedded inside. The family friends who gave it to me died tragically many years ago, but their gift has resonated with me for decades. Their gift also contributed to a lifelong interest in memorizing favorite verses. Sometimes a thoughtful gift to someone will have much more of an impact than you ever imagined.

A favorite verse of mine is_____

_____

_____

_____

_____

_____

_____

MARCH 27

Now they have come to know that everything You have given Me is from You.

−John 17: 7

Another recent study reports that optimists typically live years longer than those with a pessimistic outlook. Individuals who are going through a bout of depression may see the world through a distorted lens that looks for the worst to happen - catastrophic thinking. Or they may just maintain a dismal outlook on the future: What's the use? My luck is always bad. Nothing ever works out for me, etc. This kind of destructive thinking is not only bad for our future goals, it's *really* bad for our health. Any time you catch yourself or a friend talking like this, back it up and turn the phrase around to an expectation of something good coming your way. For example: I know this is all going to work out, and I'm really looking forward to seeing how it happens. And never stop believing in miracles! They happen all the time.

An achievement today is_____

_____

_____

_____

MARCH 28

Pray then, in this way....
– Matthew 6: 9

There have been scientific studies conducted to test the efficacy of prayer. In Dr. Larry Dossey's famous book, *Healing Words,* we learn about some of these. In some studies, hospital patients were prayed for by voluntary, outside participants in the study, and other patients were not. But the patients were not informed of this. And yes, the patients who were prayed for improved more rapidly than the others. This book is filled with amazing stories regarding prayer and "nonlocal" qualities of the mind. (Stories of distant thought communication and even shared dreams.) I personally have experienced startling examples of this with my mother, daughter, and various close friends.

Experiences like this I have had are_____
_____
_____
_____
_____
_____
_____
_____

MARCH 29

Be glad in that day and leap for joy!...
– Luke 6: 23

If we've been spending a lot of time brooding, obsessing over some hurt, or pacing with anxiety and worry, we are overdue for breaking up this cycle, and getting out of the house to have fun, help someone, explore something, or have an adventure of some kind. Depression takes up too much of our time...and it's all down time! Think about doing something you've never done before. As a mental shakeup, make it something you have not even been interested in doing before. You may be surprised at how much you enjoy whatever it is, maybe not. But the new experience may shake up some of that lethargy or listlessness that goes with depressed mood.

Something I've never done before is_____

_____

_____

_____

_____

_____

_____

MARCH 30

...the kingdom of heaven is like a merchant seeking fine pearls.

– Matthew 13: 45

We need to avoid whatever distracts us from our serenity. In various 12-Step groups we often hear about *turning it over to our Higher Power*. Often we need to get out of our own way, stop struggling, and wrestling with an obstinate problem and learn to identify instead with serenity. We *always* have the choice of choosing peace of mind, no matter what distress is going on in our life. Try saying it: "I am turning this over to you, Lord, because I'm tired of struggling with it." Then feel free to release it, and take the time to notice how this affects your sense of well-being. Remember too: *Solutions come to a rested mind, but run away from a tired or troubled mind.*

Something I'm tired of struggling with is_____

_____

_____

_____

_____

_____

_____

MARCH 31

…while seeing, they may see and not perceive, and while hearing, they may hear and not understand…

– Mark 4: 12

This is a reference to an Isaiah verse that you may recognize. If you are not familiar with the reference, it is: Isaiah 6: 9. If you look it up, you may become interested in studying the many links between the Old Testament and the New. Looking up these references to the Old Testament when we find them will deepen our understanding of the Bible. It's kind of like a treasure hunt, and most Bibles provide notes that make it easy to do. Remember that study is excellent brain exercise. If you don't care to study the Bible, then study something that you find interesting to get those brain cells working on something other than those same old, same old recycling and boring distress thoughts.

My favorite Bible story is_____

_____

_____

_____

_____

_____

_____

APRIL 1

Now the parable is this: the seed is the word of God.

– Luke 8: 11

Planting seeds is how we work with nature to grow our gardens and crops. The birds do their share of planting also. I've found a number of vegetables and flowers growing in my yard that I didn't plant. I also found a rare form of squash that I'd planted in my garden growing along the road over a thousand feet from my farm. The birds or the wind planted that seed. And likewise, so it is when we freely scatter seeds of encouragement around to others. Who knows where they'll take root and grow? Today plant some seeds either outside or in pots in the house and let them become a symbol for this Bible verse. And plant a seed of faith in another person (or yourself). It may grow if you give it light and keep it watered.

An achievement today is_____

_____

_____

_____

_____

_____

APRIL 2

...Draw some out now and take it to the headwaiter...
– John 2: 8

This quote from the story of Jesus turning water into wine at the wedding in Cana is just one reference to Jesus drinking wine. However, it's important to remember when going through a low period that alcohol will only contribute to lengthening a period of depression. Alcohol is a depressant. It may lift a person's spirits briefly, but the downswing in mood after it wears off can be severe. Even if you have never had a problem with alcohol, if you're depressed, avoid it like the plague. Do not drink even a small glass of wine! There are calming herbal teas readily available that will take the edge off, and not leave you worse off than you were before you drank them as alcoholic drinks will do.

An achievement today is_____

_____

_____

_____

_____

_____

_____

_____

APRIL 3

As You sent Me into the world, I also have sent them into the world.

–John 17: 18

Even our smallest acts are important. When we interact with cashiers, service people, salespeople, etc., we can create ripples of kindness by our behavior. Conversely, if we're in a rotten mood and consequently rude or surly, we can ruin someone else's day, if they're feeling vulnerable. This also causes ripples...but not helpful ones. If we treat everyone with kindness on this everyday, routine level, it is as important as the way we treat the more "important" people in our life. These routine interactions can reveal the baseline of a person's character. Maybe we're in a down mood, but maybe that other person is also, and we just put them over the edge with our bad temper, so that they'll pass it on to others, causing hurtful ripples. Once I gently asked a rude salesperson if she was having a bad day, and she burst into tears!

An achievement today is_____

_____

_____

_____

APRIL 4

For whosoever does the will of My Father who is in heaven,
he is My brother and sister and mother.

– Matthew 12: 50

If you have been let down by family members and have distanced yourself from them because of hurtful experiences, remember the above verse. You may even have a toxic family. Maybe you don't even have any family left. You may find more of a sense of family with friends than your blood relatives. You may discover a sense of family in a group you have met in a church or synagogue or elsewhere. You may feel a sense of family with a support group, whether it be a counseling group, a 12-Step, or community volunteer group, a special interest or athletic group. There are all sorts of groups that meet regularly whose members develop a close sense of camaraderie. Chess groups, musician groups, book discussion groups, drumming circles, sporting teams, and horticulture groups are just some examples. Family is a label we can apply to many more than just relatives.

Someone or a group that feels like family to me is_____
_____
_____
_____

APRIL 5

He who has found his life will lose it, and he who has lost his life for My sake will find it.

– Matthew 10: 39

After being immersed in our own problems and worries, it can be refreshing to interrupt a period of down mood by focusing our attention elsewhere. Laughter provides an immediate chemical change in body/mind. This has been shown in numerous studies. In fact, laughter has cured people of serious illnesses. Consider Norman Cousins' famous book about curing himself with laughter by watching funny movies: *Anatomy of an Illness*. If interested in reading more about how these chemical changes take place, read Candace Pert's *Molecules of Emotion*. This book explains, in layman's terms, the intricate chemical flow in our bodies and its connection with our moods. In the meantime, maybe watch a comedy, visit a funny friend, or play with your pets. Throwing a ball or Frisbee for a dog will turn a sour mood around in a hurry.

Something that makes me laugh is_____
_____
_____
_____

APRIL 6

...The things that are impossible with people are possible with God.

– Luke 18: 27

Once my daughter was stranded at an airport owing to bad weather. She was far from home and facing a delay of many hours. She had run out of money and was hungry and thirsty. She found enough money in a phone booth to buy coffee and snacks. God provides us with what we need. We need only exercise our faith that this is so. As we exercise our faith, we strengthen our faith. My daughter relied on faith, and knew she would not go hungry for long. "That's always the way it is," she reported. "Something always happens like that at the last minute when I'm in need."

A saving experience I've had is_____

_____

_____

_____

_____

_____

_____

_____

APRIL 7

Man shall not live on bread alone, but on every word that proceeds out of the mouth of God.

– Matthew 4: 4

We can receive impressions, insights, new ideas, and creative inspiration in many ways. Through our environment; something a stranger says; a phrase that stands out for us in a book or magazine; and through nature. To this point, an interesting book about one woman's uncanny message from nature is: *Gift of the Red Bird* by Paula d'Arcy. The author describes how a cardinal kept interacting with her in a most remarkable, meaningful way when she was going through a personal struggle, and how much this bird meant to her. Keep your eyes open for inspiration around you. You may be surprised by what you discover if you stay alert.

Inspiration that came to me from an unexpected source

_____

_____

_____

_____

_____

_____

APRIL 8

...Gather up the leftover fragments so that nothing will be lost.

– John 6: 12

If we have suffered losses, and we are grieving over our loss, it can be helpful to remember what we do have, and focus on that. Making a list of everything for which we are grateful can help us to switch our internal dial over to a sense of well being. If you're keeping a journal you can make your list there. If you're not keeping a journal yet, buy a notebook and begin today. There are many beautiful journals for sale but they can be intimidating to some people just because they *are* so beautiful a person may not want to write in them! A person may be more willing to write in an inexpensive notebook, and thus be more likely to make journal writing a habit. Journaling helps us sort through our feelings, and gives us new insights.

An achievement today is_____

_____

_____

_____

_____

_____

APRIL 9

...If anyone wishes to come after Me, he must deny himself, and take up his cross and follow Me.

– Matthew 16: 24

In a dream, Jesus was leading me along the western levee of the great Atchafalaya Swamp, near where I live in Louisiana. The dream affected me so much, I wrote a song about it: *Jesus Drives a Pickup Truck*. Two of the lines in the song are: "Now I always keep his lights in view as I travel down the road. And I do feel a whole lot better cause I do what I was told." We can receive guidance and inspiration in dreams. There are stories of dream guidance all through the Bible. The more we record our dreams, the better we will remember them. Dream descriptions can go right into that notebook where we journal every day, or we can keep a separate dream notebook.

A guidance or prophetic dream I've had is_____

_____

_____

_____

_____

_____

_____

APRIL 10

…My Father is working until now, and I Myself am working.

–John 5: 17

Work is good! Work tires us physically so we can sleep well. Work exercises our muscles and contributes to a healthy cardiovascular system. Work takes our mind off brooding thoughts. Work achieves something so that we can enjoy a sense of pride in accomplishment. Heavy lifting strengthens our bones. Work aids the flow of mind/body chemicals that make us feel good. Yet when in a depressed mood, we may not feel energetic enough to walk across the room. Then as we get more and more behind on jobs we should be doing, we feel the weight of all the things left undone blocking our energy flow even more. *Any* steps we take, however, to begin a needed job will help improve mood and maybe even set up the momentum needed to keep going and finish up. And keep up that inner mantra: *One Day at a Time!* We can do what seems impossible if we take it one day at a time.

An achievement today is_____

_____

_____

_____

APRIL 11

...When I sent you out without money belt and bag and sandals, you did not lack anything, did you?...

– Luke 22: 35

We *want!* We want things to fill our yearnings for peace of mind, serenity, and God. So we buy, or we wish we could buy. We live in a consumer society, where even our government encourages us to buy more to help the economy. It's not just the advertisers anymore! But the truth is, we need so little to be happy. And things will never make us happy. If you tend to talk yourself into "shopping therapy," give it a rest. It's not the way to go. And often it will make things a lot worse if it hurts you financially. Instead of "buying therapy," try "giving therapy." Keep putting things into the giveaway bag (or maybe the rag bag). And take time to enjoy the lighter mood that goes along with releasing and getting rid of all that stuff.

An achievement today is_____

_____

_____

_____

_____

_____

_____

APRIL 12

…What are these words that you are exchanging with one another as you are walking?…

– Luke 24: 17

People tend to stay clear of those who are downcast and sad. People naturally gravitate to funny people and people of good cheer. When we're in a down mood, it's hard to be cheerful. However, we can remember to talk about something other than our worries or complaints. We can save those for a counselor, or journal, or our prayers. There's nothing wrong with expressing our feelings to a trusted friend. But balance is the key here. Once we've expressed what we feel badly about, we can turn it around, and listen to others. They may have hurts to express also. Draw them out with questions. This will help with being self-absorbed, which is an unhelpful characteristic of depression.

An achievement today is_____

_____

_____

_____

_____

_____

APRIL 13

…You have hidden these things from the wise and intelligent and have revealed them to infants…

– Luke 10: 21

Spiritual truths can be obscured by intellectualizing. People too much "in their head" can miss out on a great deal. We have a saying in 12-Step groups, "You can't be too stupid to get this program, but you might be too smart to get it." Visualizations can help us take a rest from all that endless thinking. Visualizations are restful, healing, and refreshing. One such peaceful scene that works well for me is a cabin in the woods on a Northern lake. There is a long dock down the path from the primitive cabin. There is a red canoe lying on the bank. There are silver fish jumping in the lake, making ripples that keep spreading out in circles. There is a strong scent of pine from the woods surrounding the lake. Visualizing this gives me instant relaxation. You can use an image from a place you've been, or make up your own peaceful scene, then notice how this makes you feel as you enjoy it.

A scene I like to visualize is_____

_____

_____

_____

APRIL 14

He who is not with Me is against Me; and he who does not gather with Me, scatters.

– Luke 11: 23

Our thinking may be scattered, and our organizational abilities may suffer when going through a down period. Memory also. It can be helpful to put everything back in the same place we always keep it, and not put it in a new place. It can help to keep lists of what's needed on errands. It can help to keep a notepad by the phone, and it's wise to secure extra car and house keys. Journaling helps with this also. The very act of daily writing in our journal leads to better organizing, because it develops the mind-set that we can rely on our self to follow through with best intentions.

An achievement today is_____

_____
_____
_____
_____
_____
_____
_____
_____

APRIL 15

...you are worried and bothered by so many things.

– Luke 10: 41

Some people are always busy. Busy at their chores, busy at career, and busy socializing. Often they can be critical of those of a more contemplative nature. In the Martha and Mary story, we learn that contemplation, devotion and prayer are more important than all that activity. However, brooding and allowing racing, anxious thoughts to stall us and sap our energy don't count as contemplation! If that be the case, we need to interrupt all that mind static and teach ourselves how to short-circuit this brooding and misery and focus our attention on something else. This will change the chemical flow in body/mind and increase our sense of well-being, so we can get moving forward again.

An achievement today is_____

_____
_____
_____
_____
_____
_____

APRIL 16

… stop making My Father's house a place of business.
–John 2: 16

People who think anger is a "bad" emotion should remember that Jesus expressed anger. Our anger tells us when something is wrong. There are many feelings under the anger umbrella: resentment, jealousy, envy, irritation, annoyance, fury, rage, frustration, fear, etc. It's therapeutic and healthy to express these in a non-threatening way. People with poor anger management skills, however, can cause destructive scenes. They can get into trouble with violent outbursts. They can lose friends owing to unpredictable tantrums. Knowing how to express our anger to the right people in safe and effective ways is a coping skill that steadily improves with practice. This is something else that journaling helps. Writing it down not only expresses it, but also changes it.

Something I wrote down today is_____

_____

_____

_____

_____

_____

APRIL 17

Give, and it will be given to you...
— Luke 6: 38

Giving always feels good. I believe Jesus tells us to give, not for the receiver, but for *us*. When we give, we are expanding. When we hang on to something, we are contracting. When we're in an expanded mood, we feel good and have good will towards all. When we're in a contracted mood we don't feel particularly generous toward anyone. We may feel judgmental and burdened with a multitude of dislikes. Giving doesn't just mean giving possessions, it also means giving of our time, or even a smile. And it will help us interrupt that self-absorbed brooding so typical of a depressed mood.

An achievement today is_____

_____
_____
_____
_____
_____
_____
_____
_____

APRIL 18

For what will it profit a man if he gains the whole world and forfeits his soul?...

– Matthew 16: 26

Sometimes we can feel depressed if we're not living in a manner true to our nature, and true to our soul. Depression can be a signal that change is needed. Maybe a job has a higher monetary gain than one that is more in line with our self-actualization. A man I know was deeply depressed after being fired from a most prestigious job. I encouraged him to go do what he had always wanted to do. It was scary, but he did it, and is overjoyed to this day because he's become a successful stage actor. He took a huge risk by going to a major city and following his dream, and he's so happy today that he did!

Something I've always wanted to do is_____

_____

_____

_____

_____

_____

_____

APRIL 19

...your faith is great...
– Matthew 15: 28

Jesus here was congratulating and rewarding a woman who had great faith that He would heal her. Practicing faith that we will come out on the other side of depression brings many benefits. It will counteract the natural tendency of a depressed mood that the gravity and gloom will go on and on. It won't, if we believe it won't. However, some people cling to their depressed mood because they are so used to it, it feels familiar to them, and they are almost afraid to feel good again! Don't get *used* to feeling depressed.

It feels a whole lot better to come fully back to life again and reclaim our joy.

An achievement today is_____

_____

_____

_____

_____

_____

_____

_____

_____

APRIL 20

...Do you not understand this parable?...

– Mark 4: 13

One way of practicing our faith is to repeat the 12-Step saying: *Let go and let God.* Sometimes we have been trying too hard and making life more difficult than it really needs to be. We've been getting in our own way with self-doubt and fear. *Let go and let God* is a prescription for easing up. Remember it and repeat it silently or out loud often. Take note of how you feel when you repeat it. We need reminders often during the day to keep in tune, so write out helpful quotes and post them where you can see them often. Here's a good one: *This too shall pass.* And also during the Passover Season, we are reminded that God's protection surrounds us.

A helpful quote for me is_____

_____

_____

_____

_____

_____

_____

APRIL 21

Come to Me, all who are weary and heavy-laden, and I will give you rest.

– Matthew 11: 28

It's useful to mentally scan our body frequently. In this way, we find places we are holding tension and release those tight areas. For example, some of us hold irritation or other stress in the back of our neck, others in the lower back, or stomach. This can lead to headaches, stomachaches, backaches, fatigue, etc. As we relax those areas, we can also imagine them growing warmer. Also, as we scan our body, we may discover we are slumping and straighten our spine. If we're in a down mood, we may be aggravating it with a defeated posture that looks like we've been worn down. Standing or sitting straight will at least *look* like our mood is improving. And we will feel the difference right away.

A place I hold tension is_____

_____

_____

_____

_____

APRIL 22

and a man's enemies will be the members of his household.

– Matthew 10: 36

If someone you love is acting "crazy", and they use alcohol or drugs, consider the following. During those years I worked in a psychiatric hospital, I also worked at times on the addictions unit. Ed, one of our most experienced alcohol/drug counselors taught that even though a person is acting crazy, or thinks they're going crazy; watch how quickly they become sane when they stop ingesting drugs and alcohol! If you are affected by someone close to you who is abusing drugs or alcohol, get to an Al-Anon meeting. They are very welcoming, and the meetings will help you respond much more effectively to the alcoholic or addict in your life.

An achievement today is_____

_____
_____
_____
_____
_____
_____
_____

APRIL 23

He who is not with Me is against Me...
– Matthew 12: 30

All Jesus' directions and teachings are to help us get on God's channel. And if we're on God's channel, we will know it because of the way we feel. If we're feeling lousy, we are most definitely not on God's channel. We need to tune up. Musicians take great care to tune up before practicing, and when they are getting ready for a performance. They are not satisfied with being just close to being in tune. They take the time to be precisely in tune for their own instrument, and with the other members of the band or orchestra. There are things we can do to get in tune each day and all during the day. If we find we are going "flat" again, we need to tune up.

Ways I tune up are_____
_____
_____
_____
_____
_____
_____
_____

APRIL 24

...Follow Me, and allow the dead to bury their own dead.
— Matthew 8: 22

Ten years ago, a nurse friend, Barry, took the time to give me a tape which stressed how so often when we go through a rough time, we are going to come out of it at a higher level then we were previously. She knew I was going through a rough time, and she brought me that very important tape. I felt so downhearted and forlorn that I could barely summon the energy to get off the couch. However, I listened to that tape over and over until I really got that message. And then, incredibly, I not only got the message, I had a major breakthrough, and came up with a fantastic idea which changed my life completely. You never know how far reaching the help you give a friend or a stranger will be, or how much it will change the course of their life.

An achievement today is_____

_____

_____

_____

_____

_____

APRIL 24

*For everyone who asks receives, and he who seeks finds, and
to him who knocks it will be opened.*

– Matthew 7: 8

If you don't like the way some people are treating
you, remember this: *We teach others how to treat us.*
If you feel disrespected, sound off about it. If you
feel offended, let the person know. If you feel condescended to, say so. We don't have to be ugly about it.
We can let the other person know in a civilized tone
of voice. And every time we do speak up for ourselves, we will do much toward elevating our mood
and raising our confidence meter.

A time I spoke up for myself was_____

_____

_____

_____

_____

_____

_____

_____

_____

_____

APRIL 25

*...for He causes His sun to rise on the evil and the good,
and sends rain on the righteous and the unrighteous.*

– Matthew 5: 45

Judging others will not help elevate our mood. Being
unforgiving will not help our mood to lighten. We're
instructed to forgive to help *us*. So we can feel the
serenity and peace of mind that is our birthright. Our
natural way of being. And if our natural way of being
is clouded over by resentments and unforgiveness, we
can dissipate that cloud by praying for help with the
unforgiveness. No matter how many times it takes, we
can continue to pray for help with this, if we can't seem
to do it on our own. We've seen many accounts of people (whose family member has been murdered), forgive the murderer. If they can do it in such an unthink-
able situation, we can do it for whatever it is we may be
dealing with.

Someone I need to forgive is_____

_____

_____

_____

_____

_____

APRIL 26

Have you understood all these things?...
– Matthew 13: 51

Those who "over think" or intellectualize much of the time probably are spending too much time in their heads, and can often be unaware of their true feelings. In the mental health field this is referred to as "being numb below the neck." Massage or dance class, martial arts, yoga, Feldenkrais sessions, (truly life-changing if suffering from chronic pain,) acupuncture, athletics, and Reiki, are just some examples of ways to expand our awareness of what is going on in our bodies. It's not always easy to "get out of our heads," (and into our hearts) when troubled, but it can definitely be done with a little help.

An achievement today is_____

_____
_____
_____
_____
_____
_____
_____

APRIL 27

...You shall love your neighbor as yourself.
– Matthew 22: 39

And it's important to be kind, not only to the neighbor, but to our self. If we want to move towards goals, and we're struggling to buoy up the energy to make progress, then it's important to reward our self when we do manage to get something done. Something as simple as an ice cream cone or a Cappucino can be an effective reward. Maybe you'd rather take in a movie or hear some live music. If we make it a point to reward our self for small triumphs, we'll be more likely to accomplish even more tomorrow.

A reward I'd like is_____

_____

_____

_____

_____

_____

_____

_____

_____

_____

APRIL 28

...A city set on a hill cannot be hidden.
— Matthew 5: 14

One way to get some distance from problems and a troublesome situation is to visualize ourselves high on a mountain looking down on the town or city where we live. Breathe the fresh air from that elevated position and see how small the people, houses and streets appear. This will give us a different perspective and provide us with what is probably a much needed break from any ongoing fears or worries we may have. Remember that when we visualize a scene, our muscles actually believe we are there. We can relax quickly because of this.

Something I distanced myself from today is_____

_____

_____

_____

_____

_____

_____

_____

_____

_____

APRIL 29

You are the light of the world...
– Matthew 5: 14

If experiencing a down mood, we can imagine the bright light of our spirit burning within. We can feel its warmth spreading throughout our body. The late Swami Muktananda, a well-known spiritual teacher from Ganeshpuri, India, asked in his writings, "If you doubt you have an inner light, then how do you think you see your dreams at night in the dark with your eyes closed?" Consider this question as you focus on your inner light, rather than any dark shadowy thoughts, and remember that light is energy, and we can draw energy from inner or outer light, whenever and wherever we wish to do so.

An achievement today is_____

_____

_____

_____

_____

_____

_____

_____

APRIL 30

...Why are you afraid, you men of little faith?...
– Matthew 8: 26

If troubled by fearful thoughts, we can memorize this Scripture quote, and repeat it often. We can also picture a protective shield of shimmering light all around us, or the person we are fearful for. We can exercise our faith and pray for help with any fearful thoughts we may have. A good affirmation for this purpose is: *I am surrounded in a cloud of God's protective Light*. If we imagine this sparkling light all around us often enough, it becomes second nature and shifts our mood from the murky shadows to feeling light and free of all that heaviness. Goodbye to the shadowy half-life and good riddance!

An achievement today is_____

_____

_____

_____

_____

_____

_____

_____

MAY 1

*While I was with them, I was keeping them in Your name
which You have given Me; and I guarded them....*

–John 17: 12

One of the ways to let go of a crushing event can be
to talk about it with a professional or a friend. A good
friend of mine lived next door to a woman whose child
was hit by a car passing through the neighborhood.
The woman called my friend every day for two months
to talk about the loss of her child. Anne knew instinc-
tively to listen intently and not offer advice. When the
woman had expressed her grief enough to somewhat
recover, the calls abruptly stopped. Anne had provided
a most important service to her neighbor by patiently
listening all those hours when others did not have the
patience to hear the woman out.

Someone hurting who I listened to is_____

_____

_____

_____

_____

_____

_____

_____

MAY 2

... many prophets and righteous men desired to see what you see, and did not see it, and to hear what you hear, and did not hear it.

– Matthew 13: 17

Don't you wish Hollywood would make a "homely" person into a star instead of the endless parade of "beautiful people?" So often the actors who don't have the Hollywood look are cast as villains in the movies. Wouldn't it be refreshingly different to see a "homely" person cast as the love interest for a change? Today look for beauty wherever it may be. You may find it in a skinny stray dog trotting along the road, a wrinkled elder's toothless smile, or dandelions pushing their way to the light through cracks in the sidewalk. Even graffiti can at times be beautiful.

Something beautiful I saw today was_____
_____
_____
_____
_____
_____
_____
_____

MAY 3

Come to Me, all you who are weary and heavy-laden, and I will give you rest.

– Matthew 11: 28

Each day if we can manage only fifteen minutes on a long-term and a short-term goal, we can be pleased with the progress. Whatever increments we do toward our goals, if done daily, add up quickly. And just like water dripping on a stone wears away the stone, we can achieve much by working on a job by increments. When we tell our self we don't want to begin something that will take a long time until we have a large block of time, we may keep putting it off for weeks. Months? Years? Better we take a short time to chip away at the job by increments. Increments add up faster than you can imagine.

An achievement today is_____

_____

_____

_____

_____

_____

_____

_____

MAY 4

They are not of the world, even as I am not of the world.

– John 17: 16

We all know the way the world sees things. The world is impressed by opulence, showplace houses, and luxury cars, not to mention beauty and fame. However, those who have achieved all this, usually report getting all that just made them want more. Human nature is hard to satisfy. I know a man who had all that, got tired of it, sold everything, and went to live in a rough cabin on a river out in Back of Beyond, so he could spend his days fly fishing. And one of the happiest people I've ever known is an old Indian who lives in a beat up trailer in the woods with two mongrel dogs. He doesn't even own a refrigerator. He's very hospitable and tells great stories if you ever get by his way. So if being down and out is driving your depressed mood, you may be influenced way too much by worldly values.

A materialistic value I have is_____

_____

_____

_____

_____

MAY 5

...Come and you will see...

−John 1: 39

People who have had cataract operations report being astounded at how bright the colors are all around them. They talk about how surprised they are by how the cataracts had so slowly changed their vision, they hadn't even noticed what they were missing. If going through a bout of depression, we also are looking through a distorted lens, and aren't aware of what we're missing. Colors may seem drab or faded to us, when they are really not. As our mood begins to lift however, we may notice colors brightening, along with our outlook on life.

A color I enjoyed seeing today is_____

_____

_____

_____

_____

_____

_____

_____

_____

MAY 6

... did others tell you about Me?

– John 18: 34

A friend of mine lost his arm in a New England farm accident. When his father visited him the first day in the hospital he asked, "What are you going to do now?" (You know how practical those New Englanders are!) What Ed did do was to become a renowned one-armed car mechanic. The word got out about how good he was so that he had constant work in his auto garage. He became so well known, that one day when taking my car there, I ran into the legendary songwriter, David Allen Coe, who had dropped off his luxury car at Ed's Garage. From that first day of his injury, his father had him thinking about what he'd do next, and Ed up and did it!

An achievement today_____

_____

_____

_____

_____

_____

_____

_____

MAY 7

…Do not fear, from now on you will be catching men.

– Luke 5: 10

If bothered by run-on, distress thinking, we can practice another thought-stopping technique. We can picture an on/off switch in our mind, then flip the switch to the off position as often as needed. These tools work better the more they are practiced.

If we keep our tools lying around on the workbench, they may get rusty and hard to use. Coping skills that we learn work best if taken out and used often. This keeps them well oiled and maintained. We can have a big collection of coping skills back on the work bench or in the tool chest, but they are most effective when taken out and used often.

A coping skill I practiced today is_____

_____

_____

_____

_____

_____

_____

_____

_____

MAY 8

…Why are you thinking evil in your hearts?
– Matthew 9: 4

When recognizing our thoughts are whirling around and going nowhere, we can also practice the technique of visualizing a STOP sign. If we're more of an audio person than a visual one, we can call out: *STOP!* (if no one is around), or say it firmly in our mind if someone is around. We become effective at managing our thoughts if we keep at it. When depressed, our thoughts don't tend to be pleasant, but rather of the disturbing, uncomfortable variety. One sure way to allow unwelcome thoughts to keep running on and on, is to not get up and get moving. If we don't like how we're feeling and thinking, then we know we need to *move* in order to get that inner mood-elevating chemistry flowing again.

An achievement today is_____
_____
_____
_____
_____
_____
_____

MAY 9

…You shall not put the Lord your God to the test.

– Luke 4: 12

If we persist in working our way through depression, making an effort despite lethargy and low motivation, I believe God will meet us halfway. Friends can exclaim, "Snap out of it!" until the cows come home, but it won't do any good. *We* have to dredge up that little bit of resolve from deep within and build on it. It's like that houseplant you thought was withering, but then you see a tiny green leaf just beginning to poke its way out. And then you're so happy, you keep an eye on it, and nurture that plant right back to health. Here's another one from Nurse Patsy: *You have to make your own life! No one else is going to do it for you.*

An achievement today is_____

_____

_____

_____

_____

_____

_____

_____

MAY 10

...foxes have holes and the birds of the air have nests, but the Son of Man has nowhere to lay His head.

– Matthew 8: 20

Another story of overcoming a terrible accident is the famous one of the drummer from the rock band, Def Lepperd. Rick Allen lost his arm because he let it hang out the window of a car and another car passed too closely. This incredible man is still a famous drummer, and works with a specially designed drum set. But this didn't happen overnight. Major hurdles can take time; however, it *is* in us to find a way. It *is* in us to explore different options. We need to reach out, get the help we need to overcome whatever it is, and nurture that tiny green leaf that's growing within us.

Something I have overcome is_____

_____

_____

_____

_____

_____

_____

_____

_____

MAY 11

…Did you not know that I had to be in My Father's house?

– Luke 2: 49

His parents were looking all over for him, and young Jesus was in the temple going about His life work. It's said that people who are doing what they see as meaningful work are much less vulnerable to depression. So, when you are brainstorming your next move, bear this in mind. By the way, if brainstorming to find a new direction in your life, always keep a notebook handy. Useful ideas may pop into your head and if you don't write them down right away, you may forget them. And remember when brainstorming, all ideas are okay. Don't fail to write down an idea because it seems frivolous or too far out. Brainstorming means including *all* the ideas pertinent to the problem.

Meaningful work for me is_____

_____

_____

_____

_____

_____

_____

_____

MAY 12

...there were many widows in Israel in the days of Elijah, when the sky was shut up for three years and six months, when a great famine came over all the land.

– Luke 4: 25

We may feel as though we're in a drought when working our way through a depressed period. Our inner landscape may be quite arid. If part of our lousy mood has to do with needing a job, then our job *is* to go job hunting. Getting up, dressed, and out on the job hunt is good for any mental distress, because it demands that we look our best as we meet and greet prospective employers. Job hunting is a learning experience. We can learn a lot about all kinds of different workplaces and people by being actively on the job hunt. And it's good for our inner feel-good chemicals because we're *moving around*. We can do lots of different things. Remember Kevin Spacey in the movie, *American Beauty?* He lost his prestigious job, but was willing to work temporarily in a fast food restaurant to generate income. Keep up the hunt because giving up and resigning yourself to being unemployed leads to lethargy and a sense of defeat. Unless you are one of those innovators who thinks up a new home industry for themselves.

An achievement today is_____

_____

MAY 13

...Friend, your sins are forgiven you.

– Luke 5: 20

One morning while I cooked breakfast, a red cardinal was thrashing himself against the kitchen window. Realizing he was attacking his reflection, I quickly taped blank paper over the panes so he would stop hurting himself. So it is with us when we allow our thoughts to stray into the *I shoulda, woulda, coulda* Field of Futility. When we get bogged down in beating up on ourselves, we are like that cardinal, uselessly bashing our heads against a shadowy nonexistent intruder. And like the cardinal, we are hurting our self by attacking what is only our own reflection.

An achievement today is_____

_____

_____

_____

_____

_____

_____

_____

_____

MAY 14

Give, and it will be given to you...
– Luke 6: 38

My grandmother worked for the Salvation Army, which gave me an early appreciation for their work. I have always loved "The Sally," and just seeing their red sign or someone in that handsome black and crimson uniform makes me feel good. I was happy to work for them at one time, and would recommend their services, including their church services, to anyone passing through a rough time. If it's crossed your mind to do some volunteer work to help get your mind off whatever is troubling you, you might consider lending the Army a hand.

An achievement today is_____

_____

_____

_____

_____

_____

_____

_____

_____

MAY 15

But the one who has heard and has not acted...
– Luke 6: 49

When struggling with procrastination, become aware of how you avoid starting a job that you know has to be done. Believe me, I am an *expert* at this. If still at the beginning of a lengthy project like this calendar book for instance, I can suddenly think of more things I just have to do first. That closet! I *must* straighten it out. Or, I just *have* to give the dog a bath right now! However, once there's momentum going, and I really get some traction on a project, then Tunnel Vision sets in, and everything else gets really neglected. (I'll eat the weirdest suppers so as not to take the time to go to the store. Ever try Ramen noodles and canned beets? Or raw onion sandwiches?) Tunnel Vision can be very effective in achieving our goals.

An achievement today is_____

_____

_____

_____

_____

_____

_____

MAY 16

...describe what great things God has done for you...
– Luke 8:39

What would the bumper sticker of this time in your life say? Life Sucks? If I Didn't Have Bad Luck, I Wouldn't Have Any Luck At All? If so, try this one instead: *Everything I need comes to me!* If feeling downcast, you might not believe it, but if you keep affirming this, you will be surprised at how very fast you start to find out it's really true. Remember that Rolling Stones' line: "You can't always get what you want, but you get what you need"? Sing that as an affirmation often, and stay alert for evidence affirming how true it really is.

Something I want but don't need is_____

_____

_____

_____

_____

_____

_____

_____

_____

MAY 17

... they are choked with worries and riches and pleasures of this life...

– Luke 8: 14

If you're feeling "choked by anxiety," consider listening to a tape each day that eases those fearful thoughts. There are a multitude of relaxation tapes, nature sounds, clinical hypnosis tapes, and other anti-anxiety tapes available in book stores, second-hand stores, and libraries. These can be very effective for learning to manage any anxious thoughts. We can become frozen in place with anxiety, and these sorts of tapes can unthaw us, so that we want to get moving again.

An achievement today is_____

_____

_____

_____

_____

_____

_____

_____

_____

_____

MAY 18

...Someone did touch Me, for I was aware that power had gone out of Me.

– Luke 8: 46

Touch. Candace Pert in her book, *Molecules of Emotion*, talks about the importance of touch for our optimum well being. If you have someone to embrace, hug, hold hands with, and feel the warmth of closeness with, that's terrific, but if you don't at present, then hug your dog or cat. If you don't have a pet, then think about getting one. If you're allergic to pets, then consider getting a massage. If you can't afford a massage, then get back with me, and I'll think of something else. Oh, wait a minute! You can go to a 12-Step meeting, they always hold hands when reciting the Lord's Prayer at the end.

An achievement today is_____

_____

_____

_____

_____

_____

_____

MAY 19

Let these words sink into your ears....

– Luke 9: 44

If somewhere in the back of your mind, you have the notion to "just check into a psych hospital," to rest up and recuperate from whatever hard ball life has thrown at you, then understand this: Those psychiatric nurses won't let you sleep or lounge around. They will be telling you early in the morning "Get up, get your shower, get dressed, make your bed, and get down there for breakfast." It's like being in the Army. "I'm too worn out to get up," won't cut any ice with any nurses I've known. And after breakfast, they'll keep after you to attend every meeting, every group, and every activity all through the day until suppertime. And there'll be still one more evening group after that! So self-coach and repeat as needed: *Get up, get your shower, get dressed, make your bed, and get to breakfast!* (Very, very important instructions by the way.)

Some self-coaching I did today was_____

_____

_____

_____

_____

MAY 20

I know your tribulation and your poverty, (but you are rich)…

– Revelation 2: 9

Remember when Willie Nelson had all that trouble with the IRS involving a million or better in back taxes? He said at the time that having a lot of money brings as many problems as not having much of it. He said he knew what he was talking about, because he'd been broke for a good portion of his life, and he knew all about what that was like. So, if money has anything to do with you being downhearted, remember what Willie says. I know when people say, "It's only money," doesn't help much if you're having trouble paying the electric bill. But, I find Willie's comments valuable in order to keep a perspective on the topic of money.

An achievement today is_____

_____

_____

_____

_____

_____

_____

MAY 21

...I am He who searches the minds and hearts...
— Revelation 2: 23

There are millions of prescriptions written for antidepressants every year in the United States. They can be life savers for individuals who are suicidal or otherwise severely depressed. Yet it's no secret that a great number of people could be working their way out of a low period without taking medication. I had a boss once whose vet prescribed antidepressants for her parrot because the parrot became agitated when she left for work! The decision to take medication is between you and your doctor. Any moves you make toward exercise and getting those natural chemicals or "opiates of the brain" flowing in your body will help you feel better, whether you choose to be medicated or not.

An achievement today is_____
_____
_____
_____
_____
_____
_____
_____

MAY 22

...The time is fulfilled, and the kingdom of God is at hand...

– Mark 1: 15

Another example of converting anger or other uncomfortable feelings into creative effort is Billy Joe Shaver, the famous Texas songwriter/musician. He lost his beloved wife, mother, and son in a short period of time and had to go into the hospital for heart surgery besides. He was devastated, yet kept writing songs and performing. Turning anguish into music...more alchemy. Get those feelings out somehow into creative effort. It is amazing how it eases the pain. I've written four albums of songs. Two of my songs have been picked up for feature film soundtracks. Believe me when I say, I have never written a song out of peace and light. Every song I've written has come out of some turmoil and inner distress. And do I ever feel terrific after I've worked those feelings out into a finished song!

A way I could create something out of anger is_____
_____
_____
_____
_____

MAY 23

...and they have no firm root in themselves....

– Mark 4: 17

If you've been uprooted, and you don't feel grounded, spiritual guidance can be found in many places. Pastoral counseling, books, tapes, and a multitude of pastors and rabbis on television and radio can help. If you're uprooted such that you're living in a motel or other transitional housing, little things can help to create a sense of home. As one actress put it who has to go on the road often: "If I can just make a hot cup of coffee in a hotel room, then I feel safe no matter in what strange city I'm in."

An achievement today is_____

_____

_____

_____

_____

_____

_____

_____

_____

_____

_____

MAY 24

...for you are not setting your mind on God's interests, but man's.

– Mark 8: 33

A book by the well-known writer, Fr. Brennan Manning, *The Ragamuffin Gospel*, has the theme that we all have suffered, made mistakes, and done foolish things simply because we all are human. If you've had the mistaken idea that you're somehow above messing up, then think again. Like the book says, we're all ragamuffins. And we're going to make even more mistakes before it's all over. It's the nature of the beast to make mistakes. So if you're still beating yourself up over something from the past, get over yourself. You're probably not a saint, and that's the way it goes with us humans.

An achievement today is_____

_____

_____

_____

_____

_____

_____

MAY 25

…and some of them have come from a great distance.

– Mark 8: 3

A highly regarded psychiatrist who worked with clients at the hospital, commented that people who are retired would do well to continue to work at something. If people don't work and just play, he said, their brains can turn to mush. So if you're retired, consider this. Playing golf or tennis, swimming, biking, or walking the beach is great exercise, but find some work to do every day also. George Burns said the reason he kept sharp and performed well into his nineties was because, "I get dressed and go into the office every day." Joan Rivers still keeps up with a demanding performance schedule well into her seventies and says she's going to keep it up on and on, year after year, just like George Burns because, "This is what I do!"

An achievement today is_____

_____

_____

_____

_____

_____

MAY 26

But if anyone walks in the night, he stumbles, because the light is not in him.

–John 11: 10

A person experiencing a low mood may not be paying attention to what they are doing because they are caught up in gloomy thoughts. This preoccupation can lead to accidents while driving or walking. A fender bender, traffic ticket, or sprained ankle during a down period is the last thing we need. Stay alert and use a favorite coping skill to shut down those worrisome thoughts. Plan as best you can so as not to hurry anywhere. Hurrying has probably led to most accidents. If you think you might be a bit late for an appointment, don't rush, just call ahead and say so. (If it's a doctor's office, they're going to make you wait anyhow.) This takes the pressure off, so you can stay safe.

An achievement today is_____

_____

_____

_____

_____

_____

MAY 27

...How many loaves do you have?...

– Mark 8: 5

The answer to Jesus' question was seven. And it is reported that we can only juggle seven things in our mind at the same time. So when getting ready to run errands, if there are more than seven things you want to remember, be sure to make a list. (Depression affects our memory, so don't worry if you can't remember seven things at a time.) Keep a pad handy for a list anyway to help keep your mind clear. And be sure to reward yourself when you accomplish those errands. An important part of self-coaching is to reward. We may encounter less resistance from that part of us that likes to say, "I don't feel like it," if there's a treat in store. And when you throw away the list you've checked off, take a moment to notice how pleasant the *closure* feels.

An achievement today is_____

_____

_____

_____

_____

_____

MAY 28

...And if a blind man guides a blind man, both will fall into a pit.

– Matthew 15: 14

Paying attention to our inner voice, our intuition, can pay great dividends. Some of my family, in the music business, were across the state at an outdoor concert. It was so far from home we'd taken rooms at a motel, and a world-renowned guitar player returned there with us and began playing for us in one of the rooms. It was a private concert, and I was thrilled because I love his music. However, my inner voice suddenly told me to get home. Feeling the urgency of this, I tore myself away from the music. It took several hours to get home, but when I arrived, I saw smoke billowing from the cottage next to my house. Steve, my tenant, had fallen asleep while cooking his supper, and the burning pork chops in the skillet had created so much smoke he would have died of smoke inhalation had I not listened to my inner voice.

A critical time I listened to my inner voice was_____

_____

_____

_____

MAY 29

But I do not seek My glory...

–John 8: 50

Whatever it is you want to do in your life, do not do it for the "glory" of it. Do it because it's a true expression of you. Let it come out from deep within, and do it for yourself. There's a songbird singing his heart out from a magnolia tree I can see from the window as I write this. I don't believe he cares who hears him or not, or whether they like his song or not. But that song's coming out regardless. He can't *not* sing that song, because that's what he does, and what he was born to do. (By the way, studies have shown that trees grow fastest when the birds sing.) Everything's so interconnected, and what we do *does* matter.

Something I was born to do is_____

_____

_____

_____

_____

_____

_____

_____

MAY 30

…Night is coming when no one can work.

—John 9: 4

When our best intentions have prevailed, and we have worked all day at whatever we had to do, we can look forward to sound sleep through the night. If going through a hard time and experiencing difficulty sleeping through the night, remember that the more physical work we push ourselves to do during the day, the more likely we are to sleep until dawn. Tossing and turning in the middle of the night is conducive to exaggerated dark thoughts, and poor sleep is a common symptom of depression. Doing hard physical work during the day is a good remedy for fitful sleep and any middle of the night anxieties. (I sleep like a rock the nights after I've mowed the grass with my push mower. This is why I don't use a rider mower.)

Physical work I did today was_____

_____

_____

_____

_____

_____

MAY 31

…Get up and do not be afraid.

– Matthew 17: 7

A neighbor's house burned down during the night owing to an electrical short. But as soon as the Fire Inspector left, Gary was clearing away the black mess, and charred debris. He never stopped working until he had his new house up and running. He took charge of his days despite the nightmare. Whatever the overwhelming job is that we have to do, we can achieve it by doing some of it each day. Gary worked at it all day every day, but even if we only manage to do a small portion of an overwhelming job, it will all get done eventually, if we keep chipping away at it by increments.

A job I'm chipping away at is_____

_____

_____

_____

_____

_____

_____

_____

_____

JUNE 1

He who has an ear, let him hear what the Spirit says to the churches.

– Revelation 3: 22

What sort of music are you hearing internally? What music is your soul making? What do you mean? Just listen. You *can* hear your soul's music. Is it slow or fast? Low pitched or high? What instruments play it best? If you don't believe me, consider this: We are an instrument. We vibrate constantly. Our eardrums vibrate as they conduct what we hear to our auditory nerve. Even if we're listening to inner music, our auditory nerve is involved. And believe it or not, sound is emitted from our ears which can be detected by sensitive recording devices. So let me ask you again, what does your soul's music sound like? (I believe the reason certain violin concertos cause some people to cry is because their soul resonates to the music.)

Some music that I love is_____

_____

_____

_____

_____

_____

JUNE 2

The one who listens to you listens to Me...

– Luke 10: 16

On the subject of music...do you ever wake up with a song you've heard before on your mind? Check out the lyrics of that song. Often the lyrics contain a message from your subconscious. Sometimes it's a song you've heard lately that keeps running through your mind, but sometimes it's one you haven't heard for a while. Honor this message and see what it's telling you. While writing this, a song started playing in my mind. It's *Don't Stop Believing,* by Journey. And isn't that a good message for all of us?

A favorite song of mine is_____

_____

_____

_____

_____

_____

_____

_____

_____

_____

JUNE 3

...Everyone who is of the truth hears My voice.

– John 18: 37

A natural response to pain is groaning. When we moan or groan we are actually creating a deeply healing, soothing vibration throughout our body. This helps cells get back in balance, and this will hasten our recovery. Place your hand over your heart or abdomen and feel the vibration as you groan from deep within. This is easy to do and very helpful, whether the pain be of an emotional or physical cause. Vary the pitch of it, and you can feel the difference in your body between the high and the low tones. Try the *OM* sound so well known and recommended by Eastern religions. Make the sound tone as deeply as the Tibetan Buddhist chants. In case you aren't familiar with these chants, this is *really* deep, like a foghorn. Take note of how this makes you feel, and repeat often during the day or night for grounding and balance.

An achievement today is_____

_____

_____

_____

_____

JUNE 4

The Spirit of the Lord is upon Me, because He anointed Me....

– Luke 4: 18

If we're experiencing a depressed mood, this is a symptom of some kind of imbalance in our life. An effective antidote for this is to practice some kind of physical balance daily. If you're familiar with a few yoga poses to improve balance, practice these. If you are not familiar with yoga, then stand on one leg for as long as you can, then follow this up with repeating the pose on the other leg. As you practice, stay near to a counter or something you can grip if you should lose your balance, and if you do, reposition yourself, and then keep at it. This is good therapy for emotional balance as well as physical balance. If you can't stand on one leg owing to a physical condition, then adapt the concept to your capabilities.

An achievement today is_____

_____

_____

_____

_____

_____

JUNE 5

...Why does this generation seek for a sign?.....
– Mark 8: 12

Movie therapy can help us if we're feeling down-hearted. If you care to do this, select movies that portray people overcoming hardships, devastating events, or undesired life changes. Adventure movies can be inspiring to those who are floundering and stuck and afraid to take the risk of doing something that they really want to do, but have been afraid to try. Hollywood has produced an abundance of movies of people overcoming desperate situations. While we all have different tastes, some of my favorites are: *The Apostle, Tender Mercies, Crazy Heart, True Grit, Winter's Bone, Places in the Heart, The Edge, Passionfish,* and *The River Wild.*

Movies that have inspired me are_____
_____
_____
_____
_____
_____
_____
_____

JUNE 6

... And He was transfigured before them...

– Mark 9: 2

We can program our self through repetition to react to a certain place we use for regular renewal. If you return habitually to this same spot for your contemplation, meditation, or prayer, you can reap the rewards of instant serenity and fresh ideas and insights. Use this place to recharge your batteries, get back in tune, and otherwise revitalize that same old, tired, stale thinking. In the famed Castanada books, the old Indian, Don Juan, called this a *power spot*. He recommended exploring different parts of the house for the place that felt right. It might be even be outside the house. Investigate this concept for your special spot. (I have several; one of them is in the loft of the barn.)

A power spot in my house is_____

_____

_____

_____

_____

_____

_____

JUNE 7

...for you are not setting your mind on God's interests, but man's.

– Mark 8: 33

I perceive my thoughts as coming in from the left side of my brain. If these thoughts are counter-productive and unwelcome, I mentally put up one of those neon bright yellow police tapes that read: CRIME SCENE, DO NOT CROSS! This is one of many techniques that can help with intrusive thoughts, and it works very well for me. These thought-monitoring skills will assist us in paying attention to what is happening now, today, and help us to observe the details and events going on around us with more clarity. Worry or anxious thoughts about past or future distract us from what is going on the Here and Now and can lead to all sorts of accidents. And that's a crime, so put up the yellow crime scene tape and catch up with today...where we're all better off!

An achievement today is_____

_____

_____

_____

_____

JUNE 8

...Why are you afraid, you men of little faith?. .
– Matthew 8: 26

If experiencing an emotional storm within, we can visualize the scene described in the rest of this verse: *Then he arose and rebuked the winds and the sea; and there was a great calm.* Picture Jesus rebuking that storm within you, and feel the resulting calm. Notice how the winds stop raging in your inner landscape, and the waves cease crashing on your inner shore. See Jesus standing tall with arms outstretched. *Peace. Be Still.* Rest for a moment in the aftermath of that emotional storm and feel the difference in your internal landscape. And, just like the aftermath of a thunderstorm, the world seems brighter and quieter after the passing of an emotional storm.

A calming image for me is_____

_____
_____
_____
_____
_____
_____

JUNE 9

… It is not those who are healthy who need a physician, but those who are sick.

– Matthew 9: 12

Some people suffer from agoraphobia and will not leave their house. They fear going out into the world. A woman I know was in therapy for this condition. The therapist had finally convinced her to run at least one errand. So she went to the bank, and that day, wouldn't you know it, she was there just in time for a bank robbery! Well, bizarre things happen; she wasn't hurt, and she did keep working by increments on overcoming her fears. Whatever it is we're working at overcoming, we may have setbacks, but that doesn't mean we can't keep persisting. And that includes a depressed mood. If we continue to practice our coping skills, and keep *moving*, we will overcome.

An achievement today is_____
_____
_____
_____
_____
_____

JUNE 10

I glorified You on the earth, having accomplished the work which You have given Me to do…

−John 17: 4

Life is bursting forth all around us in a radiant abundance. Fish grow in roadside ditches because birds dropped fish eggs there. Green shoots shove their way up into the sun from the most unlikely places. Potatoes sprout in our refrigerator crisper. Plants grow in rain gutters between cleanings. When you detect green shoots pushing up in the shadows of a downhearted mood, get out in the sunshine and give them light to grow. Nurture our natural inclination for rebirth and growth by getting some sun.

An achievement today is_____

_____

_____

_____

_____

_____

_____

_____

_____

JUNE 11

…what woman, if she has ten silver coins and loses one coin, does not light a lamp and sweep the house and search carefully until she finds it?

– Luke 15: 8

All is Well. I was visiting my favorite church, which is in the Smokies, when a man in overalls stood in front of a tall, shiny window looking out on the brilliant autumn woods of Lookout Mountain. Sunlight cast him in a glow as he spoke slowly and with conviction. "All is well," he said, then sat down. I can still hear his deep voice say, *All is well*, at times if my thoughts have taken a wrong turn and run astray into Worry Mode. This mountain man's calm reassuring voice quickly slows and settles those runaway thoughts into quiet and peacefulness. I believe that man would be surprised to learn how many times I've recalled his quiet words, and how beneficial this memory has been for me. We never really know if what we say will connect with someone so much that they remember it over and over again…whether for good…or not so good.

Someone's words that have meant a lot to me are____

_____

_____

_____

JUNE 12

Whoever then humbles himself as this child, he is the greatest in the kingdom of heaven.

– Matthew 18: 4

You've heard that 12-Step saying: "Insanity is doing the same thing over and over and expecting different results"? We know that isolating and reviewing past hurts over and over is a recipe for strengthening any lingering dark mood. Past hurts can be exaggerated by our ego. The human ego can cause a great deal of trouble for us. If feeling low down, ask yourself how your ego is involved in all this. Being aware of distress caused by our ego can help us overcome the emotional discomfort or pain. Always remember that our ego can be the culprit a majority of the time.

An achievement today is_____

_____

_____

_____

_____

_____

_____

_____

_____

JUNE 13

...do not worry beforehand about what you are to say, but say whatever is given you in that hour...

– Mark 13: 11

Follow through. People who follow up leads and follow through on initial contacts are more apt to get results. If looking for a job, or seeking anything else, remember the wisdom of good follow through. Just like pro athletes always use follow through when throwing or hitting the ball, so we must learn to use follow through when dealing with other matters outside of the athletic world. I know a comedian who wouldn't take no for an answer and kept contacting a world-famous comedy show. The producers finally got worn down and asked him to come to their city and perform for them. Think of all those car salesmen who make persistent follow-up phone calls over and over to any likely buyers. If it didn't pay off, they wouldn't spend all those hours making those "cold calls."

Something I could follow up on is_____

_____

_____

_____

_____

JUNE 14

and if I ask a question, you will not answer.
– Luke 22: 68

Some people are self-starters, and some not so much. If you're a self-starter, then you can be glad. But if you're good at procrastination and avoidance, then consider your friends. If you're spending time with people who are also not self-starters, then think about what this influence means to you. If you know someone who *is* a self-starter, it can be helpful to spend a bit of time with them, as their daily habits may be somewhat inspirational to you. I never knew a self-starter who wasn't only too glad to point out all their strategies for getting things done. Just ask them! A self-starter friend, Barbara, reports using important lessons from Rehab. "I never lie to myself or another. I never make excuses for not doing something." If we've been letting things slide for a while, we may need a little jump start from an achiever. This can help us get into gear and get moving again.

An achievement today is_____

_____

_____

_____

JUNE 15

...they will lay hands on the sick, and they will recover.
— Mark 16: 18

Byron Janis, a concert pianist, struggled with painful arthritis in his fingers. This interfered with his career, but didn't stop his career. He did whatever he had to do to continue playing, which included an operation on his thumbs. He puts it this way: "I have the disease, but it doesn't have me." And so it is with a bout of depression. Don't allow depression to "have you." Continue to move and invite more movement into your life, however, you have learned to do that. If there's something you want to do, but you are not doing it, ask yourself this question: *How am I stopping myself?* (And why?) Becoming aware of any tendencies toward self-sabotage is the first step toward *not* self-sabotaging.

Something I am stopping myself from doing is_____

_____

_____

_____

_____

_____

JUNE 16

… the younger son gathered everything together and went on a journey into a distant country, and there he squandered his estate with loose living.

– Luke 15: 13

If we find we are wasting time worrying about lost or wasted opportunities, we may be blind to an opportunity that is right before our eyes. Stay ever alert to opportunities around you that you may be missing. Opportunities for learning, growth, career advancement, camaraderie, fun, etc. Depression can distort, even obscure our vision. We need to overcome that tendency by taking off the blinders and paying extra close attention to what is going on around us. Speaking of paying attention, I almost stepped on a water moccasin today here at the farm. Talk about the importance of paying attention to what is right in front of our eyes!

An achievement today is_____

_____

_____

_____

_____

_____

_____

JUNE 17

The thief comes only to steal and kill and destroy; I came that they may have life, and have it abundantly.

–John 10: 10

As you think of ways to introduce more movement into your life, consider activities that you may have overlooked in the past because they are not "done" by the other members of your social group. Maybe you never bowled a game or two at a bowling alley, roller skated in a rink, learned line dancing, shot a game of pool, or took martial arts lessons. Think out of the box when it comes to activities that might get you out of yourself and over yourself. If you're awkward and lousy at a new activity, you may even get some laughs out of it (or at least give others some laughs). Not being good at something is a good humbling exercise for the ego. Remember if we don't try to keep our ego humble, events will probably do it for us!

An activity I never tried is_____

_____

_____

_____

_____

JUNE 18

...be at peace with one another.

– Mark 9: 50

A friend of mine was devastated by his divorce proceedings. He was so heart broken by the whole matter, he didn't know what else to do but go out. He couldn't stand staying home and brooding in the evenings. He discovered that he loved to dance and went to places with live music so he could fast-dance every night. He reported feeling better and better as the weeks went by. The improved mood had much to do with that constant exercise, and the subsequent flow of those chemicals that we call the "natural opiates". He made a lot of friends who also loved to dance, and his whole life changed dramatically.

Something different I did today is_____

_____

_____

_____

_____

_____

_____

JUNE 19

...the sheep shall be scattered.

– Mark 14: 27

A talented woman I knew in high school left our town for New York City to study acting. The man she married became a famous movie actor, and she led a charmed life for years. That is until they lost their daughter. What could be worse? Several years after this happened, I asked her how she got through that terrible time in her life. She immediately answered, "I *never* look back!" If you are experiencing grief over the loss of a loved one, remember her brave and very firm reply: *I never look back!* I hear her words in my mind when I find myself feeling sad and missing someone I've lost, and her words always snap me back to the present moment, *where we all belong!*

Something I keep looking back at is_____

_____

_____

_____

_____

_____

_____

JUNE 20

*...I command you, come out of him and
do not enter him again.*

– Mark 9: 25

A multitude of useful books are available on the subject of Codependency. If you find your moods go up and down depending on what another person is doing or saying, then you might consider learning something about Codependency. There are support groups for this as well. Melody Beattie's books are highly respected on this subject and easily obtained in the library or book stores everywhere. There's a famous song titled: *When Something is Wrong with My Baby, Something is Wrong with Me.* I call this song, the Codependency Theme Song. Inasmuch as possible, try to disengage your feelings from what's happening in another person's life. We all have our own choices to make, and our own lives to live. We have no power over what someone else does with their life, but Codependents can get all twisted up over trying to live another's life. If you are suffering because of another's problems, and having trouble distancing yourself emotionally, you may find a Codependency group that meets in your area. If not, take the time to read one of Melody's books. Better yet, find a meeting *and* read her books!

Someone who I allow to affect my moods is _____
_____

JUNE 21

So because you are lukewarm, and neither hot nor cold, I will spit you out of My mouth.

– Revelation 3: 16

People throughout time have loved stories. There are stories for every taste. Adventure, sci-fi, mystery, action, westerns, and spy tales are plentiful in our society. We can find good books at used book stores, garage sales, libraries, flea markets, and thrift shops. Getting involved in a good story is a great way to take a needed break from whatever has been bothering us. When caught up in that other fictional world that the writer has created, we can take a vacation from our world, learn new things, and perhaps gain a new perspective as well. If we find a book that really hooks our interest, this is helpful for combating that preoccupation with self that is the mark of any depressed state. And reading a good book is excellent brain exercise. If having trouble concentrating, you may have an easier time reading a young adult book. There are some excellent ones out there, and they're usually relatively short.

My favorite kind of book is_____

_____

_____

JUNE 22

Do not judge according to appearance...
– John 7: 24

If going through a period of depression, we may find our judgment is unsound, because of the tendency for depressed people to see the down side of every situation. One way to overcome this is to frequently self check with the 12-Step acronym HALT. HALT stands for *Are you hungry, angry, lonely or tired?* It is suggested that we ask ourselves this when becoming aware of a downturn in our mood or thinking. Then if the answer is yes to any of these, take steps to do something about it. Take care of yourself, and work your support system. Remember that if we don't care for our self, we won't be much good for anyone else.

An achievement today is_____

_____

_____

_____

_____

_____

_____

JUNE 23

...Do not grumble among yourselves.

– John 6: 43

A person whose mood is downcast may find his/her aches or pains aggravated. They may be tempted to complain about this or anything else on a continuing basis. If you notice you or a friend has been complaining a lot lately, become aware of this tendency. You may also notice the complaining stops on days when you or the friend is experiencing improved mood. It may well be that the weather is influencing the discomfort. High pressure or low pressure days, rain and damp, cold and heat, all have effects on how we feel. But whatever the weather, we will experience decreased discomfort on days that we get up and around and *move!* And bear in mind what Nurse Patsy says: *Love is the ultimate pain reliever.*

An achievement today is _____

_____

_____

_____

_____

_____

_____

JUNE 24

I am the true vine, and My Father is the vinedresser.

–John 15: 1

Jesus lived in an agricultural environment, and many of his parables were based on this. There are many ways to take metaphors from farming, Each and every weed in the field or garden is taking nutrients from the plants being cultivated. And each negative thought going through our mind is draining our life energy and our joy. Pluck out each unwanted, harmful thought, weeding your mind daily, and notice how your energy shifts with the removal of each discouraging thought. And while you're weeding, remove these kinds of ANTS as well: *Automatic Negative Thoughts*. Living on a farm, I can promise you this; nothing brings out the ants like a heavy rainfall. And nothing brings out the ANTS or Automatic Negative Thoughts like a heavy, depressed mood.

A thought I weeded out today is_____

_____

_____

_____

_____

_____

JUNE 25

I ask on their behalf; I do not ask on behalf of the world, but of those whom You have given Me; for they are Yours.

–John 17: 9

Thinking errors can cause shifts in our mood as well. Some of them are: All or nothing thinking; black and white thinking; or catastrophic thinking. There are also those who *always* predict nothing will work out well. If you find yourself thinking along these lines, remember there may be plenty of alternatives to explore in the situation. Plenty of options that haven't been considered. Stay alert to these as you go forward. Try thinking out of the box. Solutions to your problems may come from ideas that are "off the wall." But if we don't stay open to new possibilities we may stay in a rut. Don't be a timid thinker; be daring, even outrageous instead! Brainstorm! As Donald Trump says, "We all have to think, so we might as well think big!"

An achievement today is_____

_____

_____

_____

_____

_____

JUNE 26

...the tax collectors and prostitutes will get into the kingdom of God before you.

– Matthew 21: 31

We are instructed by Jesus to see all people as children of God and not label or judge. Persons that society sees as throwaways may be closer to God than those who dismiss them as outcasts. If you feel you've been looked down upon, or if you find yourself looking down on another, it can be useful to remember the above quote. We never really know what is going on with another individual. We may think we do, but we really don't, and we can be shamefully mistaken. A famous writer bought a multimillion dollar home in a Florida resort. His wife, in blue jeans and a baseball cap, was ignored by the realtor who was supposed to take care of the next customer that day. She turned the woman over to the new man in the office! And was she mad later on when she found out who it was she'd dismissed as unworthy of her time!

An achievement today is_____

_____

_____

_____

JUNE 27

...Fill the waterpots with water...

–John 2: 7

Have you noticed how often water is mentioned in the Gospels? As we drink water we can remind ourselves of the spiritual water talked about so much in the Bible. We can think of water as a spiritual cleanser that is washing away all our negative, anxious thoughts, and replacing them with spiritual tonic. It's good to also remember that any amount of dehydration affects our mood and energy levels as well. To make sure I drink enough water, I like to fill a gallon jug of water in the morning so I can check on how much is gone by evening. On hot days I can easily drink the whole gallon. If you drink a lot of coffee, tea, or sodas, be aware that they are diuretics, and you will need to increase your water intake in order to make up for those drinks, if you want to stay properly hydrated.

An achievement today is_____

_____

_____

_____

_____

_____

JUNE 28

...if your eye is clear, your whole body will be full of light.
– Matthew 6: 22

Sometimes when feeling down, we may not feel the light within us, or even believe there is light within us. Here is a technique for feeling the reality of, and the warmth of that inner light. Remember the light bulb cartoonists use to indicate someone is getting a bright idea? Imagine such a light bulb lighting up your inner self. Imagine a bare light bulb turned on in your mind which banishes any gloomy, fearful thoughts that have been casting shadows on your day. And feel the warmth and energy emitting from that light spreading slowly throughout body and mind. Allow that light to burn off any lingering residue of despondency, and feel it emanating from you. Keep it up, and your eyes will shine, and your skin will glow, and so will your smile.

An achievement today is_____

_____

_____

_____

_____

_____

_____

JUNE 29

For where two or three have gathered together in My name, I am there in their midst.

– Matthew 18: 20

Are you an introvert or an extravert? Introverts recharge their batteries when alone. Extroverts become energized when among people. The more the better. They usually love a crowd, whereas an introvert will probably avoid a crowded place. But even if you are an introvert, during a time of a low mood, do not stay alone and isolated. This is counter productive and will only ensure that the mood continues. Get out of the house and intermingle with people. Even if it's only to go to the park and people watch, you are helping yourself get out of yourself and over yourself. A friend of mine tells the story of Mr. Stone, who used to meet the trains decades ago in Blackstone, Virginia. He did this without fail, rain or shine. He drove a 1939 Chrysler, and if you needed a ride home from the train station, Mr. Stone would take you home, gratis. So don't stay in the house all day. If you can't think of anything to do, go meet a train!

An achievement today is_____

_____

_____

JUNE 30

...because they are like angels, and are sons of God...
– Luke 20: 36

My friend, Jeff, had an amazing experience when he was six years old. He was sitting on the couch and started to get up to go outside when a mysterious woman stood in front of him from out of nowhere. He was so startled by this strange woman, that he hesitated and didn't walk toward the front door. At that very moment, the wheel from a car came hurtling through the front screen door and crashed into the living room. Jeff would have been knocked down and run over by that wheel had he not been stopped by the woman who had since disappeared. His guardian angel? Jeff doesn't know, but at age fifty, the event is still vivid in his mind. Always be open to the miraculous in your life.

Something incredible that happened to me is_____

_____

_____

_____

_____

_____

_____

JULY I

…My kingdom is not of this world…
– John 18: 36

Once while on a long car trip, I had drunk endless cups of coffee to stay awake. My eyelids began to droop, and the coffee didn't help anymore. I had to stop, yet I couldn't because there were no motels anywhere in sight. I wasn't willing to stop by the side of the road and sleep for fear of vulnerability. I had been listening to a John Prine tape and the last song, *As I Went Out One Evening*, kept playing again after the tape was over. And then it played again, and again. I kept checking the tape player. It had clicked off, yet the song played from beginning to end each time. By now I was wide awake trying to solve this mystery. The song wasn't playing in my mind from auditory memory; it was playing outside my head, just as it had on the tape. This went on for a good twenty minutes, just long enough for me to be totally amazed and consequently surprised back into total alertness. I was now wide awake, and able to drive the last two hours without further drowsiness, and to this day believe this event kept me safe because of guardian angels, or some other kind of divine intervention.

Something mysterious that happened to me is_____
_____

JULY 2

…Do not fear, from now on you will be catching men.

– Luke 5:10

Coincidences can happen at any time. I cherish coincidences because they remind me that God is with us and has a sense of humor besides. While walking down the street in Mexico City, I ran into a man I'd met in Orlando. Then, a few years later, I passed him in the street in Washington, D.C. Then a year or two later, I saw him again in New York City! At that point, we burst out laughing. I have not seen him since, but that doesn't mean I won't sometime in the future! This is just one example of many coincidences in my life, and I hope you have many also, because they're often so much fun to experience and tell others about. If you do relate coincidences to others, remind them that God has a sense of humor!

A coincidence I've experienced is_____

_____

_____

_____

_____

_____

JULY 3

…Go and report to John what you have seen and heard: the blind receive sight, the lame walk, the lepers are cleansed, and the deaf hear, the dead are raised up…

– Luke 7: 22

It can be helpful to experiment with slowing everything down that you do for one day. Do everything you can in slow motion. If working our way through a period of low energy owing to depressed mood, this exercise can help. It's paradoxical, but doing simple tasks in slow motion, can create the opposite result. We may find the tediousness of slowing everything down can result in our having more energy. A friend of mine whose active and outgoing spouse became disabled and cannot be left alone, has been caretaking for years. She, very sociable and active herself, finds the daily practice of Tai Chi helpful as she copes with all she has to do each day. Learning Tai Chi requires much patience, and gives new meaning to the concept of slowing down. But the practitioner will realize great rewards as it is most beneficial to body/mind and helps to stabilize mood. Caretakers need to make sure they're taking care of themselves, or they won't be able to help the one they're caring for.

An achievement today is_____

JULY 4

*...A nobleman went to a distant country to receive
a kingdom for himself....*

– Luke 19: 12

Anne Rice, the famous fiction writer, was suffering through a major depression after the death of her husband. She reports how close they had been, and how devastated she was when she lost him. Then one day she got an idea for a new book, and began to work on this new story. From that day on, she reports, the depression lifted, and she was able to fully function once more. If you think of a project that appeals to you, begin it, and watch the heavy mood dissipate as you become more and more caught up in your work.

An achievement today is_____

_____

_____

_____

_____

_____

_____

_____

_____

JULY 5

...Truly, truly, I say to you, you will see the heavens opened and the angels of God ascending and descending upon the Son of Man.

–John 1: 51

Heaven is Under Your Feet is a song my daughter, Twinkle, wrote and sings. Nurse Patsy says it another way: *Happiness is where your feet are.* We need to keep pulling our attention back to the present when we find ourselves glooming and dooming about the future, or brooding over the past. That's a huge waste of our time, because we are missing out on all the details all around us that can be so delightful. Sometimes, when preoccupied with our thoughts, we may walk right past the rosebush that has just come into bloom, and not even notice the heady perfume or the velvety red flowers. We may even miss out on the enchanting glossy hummingbird or the iridescent dragonfly that are hovering in our view. Say *Easy Does It* whenever your thoughts get off-track, and get yourself back into the Now... A.S.A.P.

Something beautiful I noticed today is_____

_____

_____

_____

JULY 6

So you men could not keep watch with Me for one hour?

– Matthew 26: 40

The hours of sleep we're getting has much to do with stabilizing our mood. If we're not getting enough sleep, we may find ourselves feeling ragged, irritable, or tense. If we're getting too much sleep, we may feel groggy and out of sorts. Whatever we've learned is the right amount of sleep for feeling good is what we want. Many have found that going to bed at the same time helps assure a good night's sleep. It's helpful also to remember that our daily exercise uses up energy that might otherwise keep us awake and fitfully tossing and turning. When going through a period of depression, sleep might be affected, and the energy available for daily exercise might be diminished. Another reason to push ourselves into going for that walk or doing some other form of exercise.

Making ourselves use up that energy every day will help us sleep deeper and for a longer period of time throughout the night.

Something I want to learn about is_____

_____

_____

JULY 7

For if you believed Moses, you would believe Me, for he wrote about Me.

–John 5: 46

Those connecting threads between the Old Testament and the New can be so interesting. A Concordance helps us to uncover many of these links between the two. If you don't have a Concordance, you might think about getting one. They really help with Bible study. If you're interested in studying something else, keep a dictionary handy. I keep one in every room of the house, otherwise, I might not bother to go find one when I need it. Remember brain exercise is as important as physical exercise, and giving the brain something to focus on other than worries helps to stabilize our mood. (By the way, brain exercise burns calories at a hefty rate. Tournament chess players can burn as many calories as distance runners.)

An achievement today is _____

_____

_____

_____

_____

_____

JULY 8

For just as the Father raises the dead and gives them life, even so the Son also gives life to whom He wishes.

−John 5: 21

Reading back through the 'Achievement Today' lines, we can see what actions we've taken in past weeks. We may find we have been advancing by some movement each day, no matter how slight. Small steps lead to larger steps. Small chunks of work lead to larger chunks. Before we even realize it, we're nearing the end of a task because of working by increments. If we walk a block, we may soon find we're walking a mile a day. And we may soon discover we feel out of sorts if we *don't* walk that distance each day as we've grown accustomed to it. Remember the earlier writing about positive addiction? Developing positive addictions in our life can bring an end to a depressed period fast. You can read more about this in Dr. William Glasser's book: *Positive Addictions*.

Something I'm positively addicted to is_____

_____

_____

_____

_____

JULY 9

For David himself says in the book of Psalms...
– Luke 20: 42

David expressed his emotions through songs that have come down to us in the book of Psalms. These have been read, memorized, and sung for all these centuries. For years I ran a poetry therapy group at the hospital, which was popular because the clients were able to express themselves through poetry or songwriting. The group read a poem, discussed it, then each person wrote one of their own. I typed these and displayed them on a hallway bulletin board which everyone (and visitors) enjoyed reading. If you're so inclined, write a poem or song lyric to express whatever you have been going through. Then take a moment to notice how this makes you feel.

Something I'd like to write about is_____

_____

_____

_____

_____

_____

_____

_____

JULY 10

Blessed are those who mourn, for they shall be comforted.

– Matthew 5: 4

Of the five stages commonly assigned to the grief process: denial, anger, bargaining, sadness, and acceptance, in which stage do you think you are regarding a loss you have had? Sometimes people remain stuck in one stage mainly because they never fully allowed themselves to experience it and work through it. One helpful way to work through a stage of grief is to write about it in your journal. Another is to act it out in some way, or talk it out. In Russia, benches are provided in cemeteries for the bereaved to sit and talk to their loved ones at the gravesites. In this way they can express what otherwise might have stayed unexpressed inside the mourner, thereby shortening the grief process.

An achievement today is_____

_____

_____

_____

_____

_____

_____

JULY 11

I will give you the keys of the kingdom of heaven; and whatever you bind on earth shall have been bound in heaven, and whatever you loose on earth shall have been loosed in heaven.

– Matthew 16:19

This is another of those links from the New Testament to the Old. Take a minute to refer back to Isaiah 27: 22, and you will see. The more we study the Word, the more we discover the many levels of Jesus' teachings. And remember, if you don't study Scripture, study something to exercise your brain daily. This aids concentration and focuses the mind on something other than mundane concerns and anxious thoughts. There are all sorts of textbooks available in used bookstores. Botany, physics, biology, history, geography, and language texts are all fairly easy and inexpensive to obtain. If we weren't paying attention in school, we can make up for it now!

Something I'd like to learn more about is_____

_____

_____

_____

_____

JULY 12

…You shall love your neighbor as yourself….
– Mark 12: 31

Our neighbor, of course, is anyone who crosses our path today. A long running column in the Baton Rouge Advocate reports kind deeds witnessed by readers. It's heartening to read about all the reports of fellow travelers who stop to offer selfless assistance with flat tires, and other car problems even in the pouring rain. And there are plenty of instances of people returning lost wallets, purses, and other articles. We may at times be dismayed at the brokenness of the world, but there are plenty of good Samaritan stories that demonstrate kindness and honesty that don't ever make the news channels.

A good deed I've witnessed is_____

_____

_____

_____

_____

_____

_____

_____

_____

JULY 13

*...When you see a cloud rising in the west, immediately you
say, 'A shower is coming,' and so it turns out.*

– Luke 12: 54

Often if going through a period of low mood, we may
keep looking down, rather than up. Preoccupied with
dreary thoughts, we may miss a great deal that is going
on in the sky. Streaks of brilliant color, cloud formations, soaring hawks all are happening above us, but if
preoccupied with our own run-on, anxious thoughts,
we don't see, and we're missing out on great beauty.
The distorted lens of a low mood diminishes our world.
Work against this by remembering to look up and all
around when outside. Absorb the beauty of sunrises
and sunsets and all that goes on in between. Then at
night, go outside and study the stars, check what phase
the moon is in. Any effort you make toward heighten-
ing awareness will improve mood.

Something beautiful I saw today is_____

_____

_____

_____

_____

_____

JULY 14

Are not five sparrows sold for two cents? Yet not one of them is forgotten before God.

– Luke 12: 6

Even if we feel we are living a sort of half life when going through a down period, we are not forgotten. Ask God to help you feel fully alive again. Then push forward by doing something you know will help to lighten your mood. There may be important *inner* work going on throughout a low period of which we are not aware. As we incorporate action into our life we will discover what that vital inner work was all about. And as we bring it into awareness, we may be excited to learn it's a whole new way of being. We may have been subconsciously reinventing our self, and discover we are off in a whole new direction. *We may find it's a better direction than the way we were going before, and worth all the discomfort and confusion of transition.*

An achievement today is_____

_____

_____

_____

_____

_____

JULY 15

And why do you not even on your own initiative judge what is right?

– Luke 12: 57

Sometimes, if going through a down period, we may find it difficult to make decisions. Even small decisions. Finding out as much as we can about whatever decision that has to be made can be helpful. Give yourself time to gather the facts, and make lists of your options if need be to help with clarity. Keep your mind clear so you can listen to your inner guidance. When it feels right, you'll know it. And if someone such as a real estate or car salesman is pressuring you for a decision, get away. Say you'll sleep on it. Always a good thing to do before making a big decision. (Also remember that not making a decision is a decision in itself.)

An achievement today is_____

_____

_____

_____

_____

_____

JULY 16

Any kingdom divided against itself is laid waste; and any city or house divided against itself will not stand.

– Matthew 12: 25

Make a support system diagram by drawing a small circle in the middle of a piece of paper. Then draw lines from the circle outward like the spokes of a wheel. Next, draw a small circle at the end of each line. In the center circle, write SELF. Then in each of the circles at the end of the spokes of the wheel, name a part of your support system.

Maybe it's a support group, maybe a counselor, a friend, athletic group, a club, or other organization. Maybe a church or synagogue. Maybe you put a hobby or other interest in one of the circles. Pets are part of our support system. Put anything that supports you emotionally or physically. Maybe a card or chess club. Then survey your diagram and ask yourself if you've been working your support system. If not, think about how you can.

I used my support system today by_____

_____

_____

_____

JULY 17

But so that you may know that the Son of Man has authority on earth to forgive sins...

– Mark 2: 10

Hymns are an important ministry also. Famous writers of hymns include Charles Wesley, (John Wesley's brother,) Fanny Crosby, and John Newton. If you are so inclined, put on a Gospel radio station or CD. A good gospel song is as good as a sermon insofar as putting across an insightful message. And of course, we mustn't forget David who composed those early hymns as a young man, which we call Psalms. And don't forget David sang those songs and accompanied himself on the harp so as to soothe King Saul. Whatever your favorite hymns may be, contemporary, or traditional, you may find your mood elevated and soothed by playing or singing some of them. And don't forget what Dr. Urbino said to Fermina when she was ill in Marquez's beloved novel, *Love in the Time of Cholera,* "Music is important to your health." So, be sure to listen to your favorite music every day, whatever it may be. *Music is God's healing love. He knows we need help from up above.* (From the song: Old Texas Picker)

My favorite music is_____

_____

JULY 18

...Do you see anything?

– Mark 8: 23

A good deal of psychological input goes into the experience of pain. We anticipate more pain and so our muscles tense. This aggravates the pain. When it comes to chronic pain, the individual needs to learn how to relax so as to nullify this tendency. The same situation exists with emotional pain. If going through a down period, we may anticipate more pain and tense ourselves in anticipation for this. If, on the other hand, we don't keep telling ourselves, "I am depressed," we may find to our surprise during the day that we are actually feeling okay, and not down-hearted after all. When discovering a less dense, lighter mood, nurture that by taking a walk or doing something that increases movement so as to keep our natural "feel good" chemicals flowing. This will lengthen the duration of improved mood.

My best times today were_____

_____

_____

_____

_____

JULY 19

...Do you have a hardened heart?

– Mark 8: 17

Studies have shown that pet owners have statistically less episodes of depression than non-pet owners. The belief is that this is a combination of the greeting the pets give us when we come home, and their great affection for us. Also the beneficial effects of touch are well known, and of course, the love that is freely given back and forth is another major factor. In addition, pets have demonstrated an uncanny ability to recognize major physical problems that are imminent in time to give warning, such as seizures and heart attacks. They let us know if intruders are lurking about. Asthma patients gain relief with Chihuahuas in the house. And recently studies have shown that cats purring on our lap strengthens our bones, apparently because of the vibration! So, if you're so inclined, rescue a pet today. You may be rescuing yourself as well!

An achievement today is_____

_____

_____

_____

_____

JULY 20

...You are not far from the kingdom of God...
– Mark 12: 34

There are so many electromagnetic waves flying about in cities from the explosion of high tech equipment, not to mention cell phones and microwaves, satellite TVs, radio waves, lasers, and X Rays. And this frenzy of invisible waves goes through walls and bathes us in disturbance constantly. Try holding up your cell phone to a tape recorder and listen to the static that is recorded if you don't quite believe just how disturbing a cell phone can be. It will also interrupt a compass. My sister-in-law left Washington, D.C. on a car trip and reported feeling peace and serenity wash over her the further away from the Beltway she drove. Of course, all those electromagnetic waves are bombarding us in small towns also, but on a much lesser scale. So if you can arrange for a trip to the country, make it a goal for the near future. Get some space between you and all that incessant electromagnetic activity.

An achievement today is _____

_____

_____

_____

JULY 21

Behold, I stand at the door and knock...
– Revelation 3: 20

When meditating, sit quietly until you become aware that your breathing is "breathing you." A difficult concept to explain, but you'll know it when it happens. When this occurs, you may find you are in such a restful state, that your thoughts have slowed way down, along with your breathing. You can help this process along by concentrating on the space just between and in back of the eyebrows. You might also scan your body and find a tingling sensation somewhere as you relax. You can actually move this tingling around at will anywhere you care to in your body or mind. You may also find a spot of warmth somewhere in your body that you can also move around at will. If you have an ache somewhere, this technique can erase it.

An achievement today is _____

_____

_____

_____

_____

_____

JULY 22

…You are mistaken, not understanding the Scriptures nor the power of God.

– Matthew 22: 29

The brain requires oxygen and water and nutrients to function well. If you are trying to solve a problem, a brisk walk can often result in a solution or at least a couple of good ideas toward that goal. The exercise is improving brain function by circulating the oxygen and increasing the flow of neurotransmitters. Hydration is extremely important for optimal brain/body function as well. Be sure to drink all those eight glasses of water we need, especially in summer when even more is needed. Dehydration can contribute to a depressed mood, and can even cause a person to faint who was not even aware they were dehydrated! Eating and drinking well also helps our brain and our mood because we are pleased we're taking care of ourselves.

A good idea I had today is_____
_____
_____
_____
_____
_____

JULY 23

...A sign will not be given it, except the sign of Jonah.

– Matthew 16: 4

Shallow breathing is a sure sign of a low and listless mood. If observing your breathing in order to make sure you are breathing deeply, visualize your in breath as clear, fresh air. Feel it all the way into your lungs, visualize it cleaning your lungs, and then visualize the exhaled breath as of a certain color...as it clears away toxins from the lungs and body. You can also do this exercise by visualizing creative thoughts entering your body on the inhale, and fearful or otherwise negative thoughts leaving your body on the exhale. Breathing therapy can be a powerful tool for improving mood...and health. *Breathe!*

An achievement today is _____

_____

_____

_____

_____

_____

_____

_____

_____

JULY 24

…It will be fair weather, for the sky is red.

– Matthew 16: 2

John Wesley, the founder of Methodism, said he felt a dynamic internal shift during a service on Aldersgate Street in London. That shift became the major turning point in his life, and from that day forward, his life as a preacher fundamentally changed. Sometimes a subtle shift in our inner landscape can occur in an instant, when something clicks, and we feel quite differently than we did before. Stay open to the possibility of a dynamic shift in your perception. It can happen at any time, and this shift within can have dramatic effects on how we are feeling. Stay alert, and watch for change. Expect it.

An inner shift I've noticed recently is_____

_____

_____

_____

_____

_____

_____

_____

JULY 25

For My yoke is easy and My burden is light.
— Matthew 11: 30

In James Galway's autobiography, he talks about growing up in the streets of Belfast, and how he discovered his love for music and the flute while still very young. He sees himself as a channel for music from God. His very entertaining book is relatively short and easy to read. It's inspirational as well, because he practiced for hours a day to become the famous and widely recognized musician he is today. Music can coax a person out of the shadow life of a dark mood. Allow one of your favorite musicians to lure you out of the shadows into the light once more. Whether it's flute or fiddle, guitar or piano, listen to some of your favorite music today, and notice how it affects your mood.

Music I listened to today is_____

_____

_____

_____

_____

_____

_____

JULY 26

But new wine must be put into fresh wineskins.

– Luke 5: 38

Another technique for dealing with intrusive memories of painful events from the past is to allow the memory to spin out, but see it in black and white rather than the natural color of it. After running the memory tape of the event in black and white, then run it again in slow motion. Then run it again in black and white *and* slow motion. This changes the memory, and creates emotional distance from it. One of the side effects of a period of low mood is to review past trauma or past sad events over and over relentlessly. This works against our regaining emotional balance, and helps block the healthy flow of the neurotransmitters that improve mood. By practicing strategies such as the above, we can change this harmful tendency. Still another technique for stopping troublesome thoughts is to visualize windshield wipers, swiping back & forth, back & forth, as they clear unwanted thoughts from your mind.

An achievement today is _____

_____

_____

JULY 27

...for she loved much...

– Luke 7: 47

Doing something to honor those we've lost can help move our grief process along. For example, I plant flowers that were favorites of people I have lost. Dahlias, violets, begonias, mums, salvia, and roses, are some of the flowers I keep in my garden to honor various people I miss. Doing something concrete in remembrance of someone we feel sad about losing changes our feelings and helps us express any emotional distress. Be creative. I lost a dear friend who used to love horseracing. There is a track fifteen minutes from my farm, and sometimes I go by there and watch a few races in memory of John.

A remembrance idea I have is to _____

_____

_____

_____

_____

_____

_____

_____

_____

JULY 28

Oh, foolish men and slow of heart to believe in all that the prophets have spoken!

– Luke 24: 25

Is there a critical person from your past whose voice you still hear? Whose voice has become your inner critic? Becoming aware of this is the first step towards silencing what may be contributing to a dark mood. If you hear nagging from your inner critic, confrontation can be helpful. Talk back to any unfair inner criticism by standing up for yourself. Such inner dialogue can be useful in finding a new direction as well. Sometimes in standing up for our own self we can gain insights that help us to see new horizons and realize what we *really* want. And it may be quite different than what is expected of us by others. Let others influence their own lives, and leave us out of their plans for our life. We are responsible for our own life direction and no one else.

Something my inner critic says is _____

_____

_____

_____

_____

JULY 29

...I did one deed, and you all marvel.

–John 7: 21

Can you think of something you can do for yourself that will be greatly appreciated tomorrow? A thoughtful gift to yourself? For example, I often make up a thermos of hot coffee at night and leave it by my bed along with an empty cup. When I wake up around five, and it's still dark, that hot cup of coffee while still in bed is very appreciated. A simple thoughtful act such as this can elevate our mood. Be imaginative. You know yourself best. Do something that will help set up a good mood for tomorrow. Any effort in this direction today can bring emotional rewards and renewed energy...and that's what we're looking for.

A gift I can give myself for tomorrow is _____

_____

_____

_____

_____

_____

_____

_____

JULY 30

…are you angry with Me because I made an entire man well on the Sabbath?

–John 7: 23

Is there someone in your social circle who is pessimistic? Complaining? Always seeing the down side or running down others? An antidote for this is to tell them you're going to write down any negative thing they say and date it. If you've been keeping a notebook close by, this should be easy to do. If you do this, you may be amazed at how quickly you can change behavior. They may still be thinking pessimistically, but at least you're making them aware of it, and dissuading them from all that thought pollution. This is doing them a service, and everyone around them a service, including you. And remember: *We teach people how to treat us.* We don't need to keep hearing all that pessimism, and it's not good for them to be dishing it out either.

An achievement today is _____

_____

_____

_____

_____

_____

JULY 31

...It was neither that this man sinned, nor his parents...

–John 9: 3

You may find some interesting things about your personality by making a diagram like this: Draw two big overlapping circles on a big sheet of paper. Make the overlapping space about a third as big as each circle. Then write all the qualities you can think of that your father had in his circle, and write all your mother's qualities in her circle. Then, in the overlap space write all the qualities you share with each of them. You can include your grandparents in this diagram also if you care to. You may find some of your personality traits or talents jumped a generation and you inherited them from a grandparent. This exercise can provide some interesting self-knowledge that you never quite saw or put together before.

A strength I'm glad I inherited is_____

_____

_____

_____

_____

_____

_____

AUGUST I

…we have done only that which we ought to have done,

– Luke 17: 10

Take notice of mood changes that typically occur at different times of the day. You may notice there are regularly occurring changes that you can alter with activity. You may notice that your mood dips at certain times during the day and evening, and you can do something at those times that will buffer this. It's well known that many people experience diminished energy during mid morning and mid afternoon. Those are good times for a protein lift to keep blood sugar levels steady. Then there are those who find twilight difficult. The French call this time: *Entre le loup et le chien,* or 'between the wolf and the dog'. If this is true for you, you may want to schedule a fast walk to accelerate circulation of oxygen and those neurotransmitters that make us feel so good. Action affects mood and creates change.

Something I did to change my mood_____

_____

_____

_____

_____

AUGUST 2

He who is faithful in a very little thing is faithful also in much…

– Luke 16: 10

The many work savers that we are accustomed to in modern times don't seem to have helped to make us happy. People born after World War II are ten times more likely to experience mood disorders than previous generations. The increased sedentary lifestyle that goes along with the computer age hasn't helped elevate moods either. There is so much to remove us from the natural environment. Air conditioning is considered to be so essential that government often provides help paying for it if individuals can't afford it. Dryers are standard equipment and hanging clothes on the line is even illegal in some communities. Personally, I use ceiling fans even on the hottest days because I don't like canned air. And I don't own a dryer because I like to dry clothes on the line. I'm for anything I can do to live closer to nature here on the farm. I even have an outhouse, but I do have indoor plumbing! The more artificially we live the more we put our natural balance in jeopardy… and that includes our moods.

Something I keep simple is_____

_____

AUGUST 3

...because they are like angels, and are sons of God...
— Luke 20: 36

In her book *Molecules of Emotion,* Candace Pert talks about a guided visualization she had in which she learned to release an abundance of beta endorphins from her pituitary gland. She says the beta endorphin is the most potent of the endorphins and she felt a rush throughout her body and brain as they were released into her bloodstream. These natural opiates help us to feel up to our natural potential, and Dr. Pert learned it's not just through exercise that we can enjoy their effects. In addition to learning to visualize the release of endorphins, acupuncture can also be directed to this purpose.

An achievement today is_____

_____

_____

_____

_____

_____

_____

_____

_____

AUGUST 4

You have sent to John, and he has testified to the truth.
– John 5: 33

As you discover more and more activities which help you to feel good, be sure to include some of these into every day's schedule. We have to make the effort to improve our mood, and by scheduling what we know will make us feel better into our everyday routine, we can construct a day in which we feel good from morning to night. If we find a day's programming that works for us, it's in our best interest to repeat it if we can, the next day. To not do something that we know will make us feel better is self-defeating. However to make the effort will result in energy flow and an increased sense of well being. The more we do what we know is good for us, the more confidence we build in our own ability to follow through. This in itself improves mood.

An achievement today is_____

_____

_____

_____

_____

_____

_____

AUGUST 5

For David himself says in the Book of Psalms, 'The Lord said to my Lord, "Sit at My right hand until I make your enemies a footstool for Your feet."'

– Luke: 20: 42

Enemies? Adversaries? There will always be people who don't care for us, but so what? As long as we are doing what we believe is right, we continue on our path. I had the good fortune of hearing Kurt Vonnegut speak at a book festival some years ago. He spoke of the importance of including an enemy in any fiction story. "They make the characters in the story behave in more lively ways," he said. So, if you think you have an "enemy," see if you're behaving in a more "lively way" because of this. One thing for sure is, we're giving them *way* too much power if we allow them to sabotage our mood by letting them disrupt our thoughts.

An achievement today is_____

_____

_____

_____

_____

_____

_____

AUGUST 6

*Then they will begin to say to the mountains, 'Fall on us,'
and to the hills, 'Cover us.'*

– Luke 23: 30

Reframing a traumatic experience can transform the individual from being a victim frozen by the event, to someone who can take up their life and be fully alive and functioning once more. During a home invasion, my friend Jeff was shot six times by a man with a rifle. He lay in a coma for four days before coming out of it with two bullets still in him that they couldn't remove. One bullet moves closer to his spine with each passing year. He reframed the nightmare and now believes God preserved him to do something. He has transformed PTSD into action. He visits the elderly and sick in our town's nursing home. He's always at Mass on Sundays at seven. He is a fabulous Cajun cook and is forever feeding his friends. He also caretakes his frail mother. Reframing can be a powerful tool for healing past trauma.

A bad experience I can reframe is_____
_____
_____
_____

AUGUST 7

*...The first and the last, who was dead, and has come to life,
says this:*

– Revelation 2: 8

When I was very young, a family friend brought my
mother a garden stake that had begun sprouting
leaves! He saved it out of his tomato patch, and mother
planted it. Out of that humble garden stake grew a
magnificent weeping willow tree. I've never forgotten
that graceful tree with its long delicate branches. As an
adult gardener, I take great pleasure in a plant coming
to life that I thought was dead. I seldom pull a plant
until it's beyond a shadow of a doubt that it's not coming back. This is also the way with a desolate lingering mood...and then one day, like the song says, *Here
Comes the Sun!,* and we feel like our old self once more.

An achievement today is_____
_____
_____
_____
_____
_____
_____
_____

AUGUST 8

...He who is without sin among you, let him be the first to throw a stone at her.

–John: 8: 7

About this woman they wanted to stone...it's still going on in some countries. This ancient practice that seems so foreign to us, so impossibly archaic...is still happening.

The Bible isn't really so ancient and distant from us after all. There is less distance between us and those old stories than we may think. And if you consider character assassination also a form of stoning, then we have such practices in our own country as well. And then, of course, we want to avoid being judgmental in our own personal life as Jesus has instructed. We are not saints! So, as they teach in 12-Step groups: *We don't need to be taking another's inventory.*

An achievement today is_____

_____

_____

_____

_____

_____

AUGUST 9

He who is a hired hand, and not a shepherd, who is not the owner of the sheep, sees the wolf coming, and leaves the sheep and flees...

– John 10: 12

Some people are unwilling to delegate any tasks to others, because they believe they are the only ones who can do the job correctly. As a result, they often feel unappreciated and forlorn because they have to do everything for themselves. Or perhaps they may feel overwhelmed with all the work they have to do, because they refuse to farm any of it out, or delegate any of it to others. If you need help with a job you need to do, explore your options. Is there maybe someone you can ask to help you? Is there someone you can hire to help you? Look at the job with the eyes of an efficiency expert and think about how you may be making the job more difficult than it has to be. Jesus delegated also!

Something I can delegate is _____

_____

_____

_____

_____

AUGUST 10

It is the Spirit who gives life; the flesh profits nothing; the words that I have spoken to you are spirit and are life.

–John 6: 63

When you accomplish something towards a goal, be sure to take at least five minutes to relish the warm feelings of *closure*. Too often when we've completed a job, we hurry on to the next thing, and don't take in the warm feeling that goes with closure. As you bask in the good feeling for a few minutes, notice how you may have also achieved new insights into how you can achieve the end goal. Perhaps the work must go on for days, weeks, or months...but each step taken towards completion can be relished for this warm humming internal feeling. And enjoying feelings of closure make it that much more likely you'll have the motivation to do even more of the job tomorrow.

Something I enjoyed completing is_____

_____

_____

_____

_____

_____

AUGUST 11

…whoever does not receive the kingdom of God like a child will not enter it at all.

– Luke 18: 17

A symptom of depression is a diminished lack of interest or enthusiasm. Remember the sense of wonder we had as children, and how we collected those treasures? Maybe kept them in a cigar box? Remember Bo Radley in *To Kill a Mockingbird?* And those treasures he'd leave for the kids in the tree? If you see something on your walks that catches your eye, pick it up and save it in a basket or cigar box just like you may have done as a child. Marbles, bird nests, shiny stones, pennies flattened on the railroad track, rusty jackknives, all could be part of a revered collection of found objects. Doing it as an adult can bring back some of the wonder and enthusiasm for your inner child and consequently turn around a dismal state of mind.

An object of interest I picked up is_____

_____

_____

_____

_____

AUGUST 12

...I will give him a white stone, and a new name written on the stone which no one knows but he who receives it.

– Revelation 2: 17

I have a whole bowl full of white stones I've picked up in order to remember this verse. What do you imagine *your* new name written on the stone would be? I like to have reminders of favorite Bible verses around the house so as to remember them often. I found a framed quote embroidered on cloth and under glass in a secondhand shop. I bought it, and that week learned a friend was going through a dreadful time in her life. I wanted to give her the embroidered verse for encouragement. I called to ask her if she could meet with me the next day so I could give her a framed Bible quote that she was sure to like. She asked, "Is it Jeremiah 1: 5?" I was startled. Out of all the many favorite Bible verses that people love to memorize and quote, she'd guessed the very one!

A favorite verse I'd like to frame_____

_____

_____

_____

_____

AUGUST 13

...Beware of the leaven of the Pharisees, which is hypocrisy.

– Luke 12: 1

The toxins in our culture are plentiful. The use of pesticides, fungicides, and herbicides is so out of hand that even farms that don't use these have traces of them in their soil. I don't permit any chemicals on my farm, and I let the fields go to native grass. I couldn't find any farmers willing to raise crops without using chemicals, so in the meantime, I let the grasses grow and hire someone to "chop" the fields once a year. So I know when I go out to hunt wild greens to eat, they are chemical free. It pains me to see television commercials showing herbicides killing dandelions because dandelion greens are delicious potent greens and have three times the Vitamin A that is found in carrots, plus plenty of other vitamins and minerals. They also help clean our liver which needs clearing from all the toxins we ingest in our chemical saturated society.

An achievement today is_____

_____

_____

_____

_____

AUGUST 14

...Someone did touch Me; for I was aware that power had gone out of Me.

– Luke 8: 46

If there's a job you used to do but can't anymore, brainstorm as to what you could do instead. I have a longtime friend who was a roofer for decades, but arthritis has made it impossible for him to do it any longer. So now he drives around and bids roofing jobs instead. An artist I know had to supplement his income, so he took a welding course and now welds for a man who creates large metal sculptures. Don't forget, when you engage in brainstorming, make a list of anything that comes to mind, no matter how far out it may be. Later on you can weed out what you don't want, but let your mind go wild in the first stages of brainstorming. It's a very useful strategy.

An idea I had today is_____

_____

_____

_____

_____

_____

_____

AUGUST 15

But he who practices the truth comes to the Light...
– John 3: 21

After experiencing a down period, we may discover our priorities have changed. We learn more from the low points in our life than the highs, and some of the lessons learned are often that some things we thought were so important just aren't anymore. We may find some things we neglected before are things we prefer to focus our energies and attention on in future. A down period produces many revelations. A shift in priorities can be life changing and life enhancing as well. As we move out of the low period and feel more and more like our self once more, we can reflect on what we learned from the gloomy period we have left behind...and we can be grateful for those important lessons.

A priority that has changed recently is_____

_____

_____

_____

_____

_____

_____

AUGUST 16

I have come to cast fire upon the earth; and how I wish it were already kindled!

– Luke 12: 49

Digging worms may seem like an unusual way to improve mood, but it's something my inner child likes to do. It's also something my adult wants to do because I have some baby chicks who love to eat worms. Besides, I live on the bayou, so worms for fishing is another reason. And it's still another aspect of the digging therapy I mentioned earlier. If it's been raining, and the ground is soggy, you may find worms on top of the ground, even without digging. If you have a mulch heap, this is a good place to look also. If you don't have a bird to feed, then maybe you could go fishing with them. Worm therapy...what a concept!

Something my inner child wants to do is_____
_____
_____
_____
_____
_____
_____

AUGUST 17

The seed which fell among the thorns, these are the ones who have heard, and as they go on their way they are choked with worries and riches and pleasures of this life...

– Luke 8: 14

Did you know cleansing your liver can improve mood? Check out liver cleansing pills at your health food store, or organic apple juice. With all the toxins we eat unknowingly, the toxins in the air, and the insidious clogging of medications and any bad habits we may have had in the past, the liver can doubtless use a good clearing out. An ailing liver is not just the alcoholic's problem. An epidemic of pollution makes it everyone's problem, no matter how much of a healthy life style they may enjoy. Greens are cleansing; and don't forget the importance of drinking those eight glasses of water a day.

An achievement today is_____
_____
_____
_____
_____
_____
_____

AUGUST 18

...You have judged correctly.

– Luke 7: 43

Drinking tea is a healthy practice. Drinking sodas is not. So brew up a pot of tea...green tea with ginger, herbal tea, or black tea. Forget the sugar. Use honey if you want it sweet, or get used to drinking it plain. (I have a friend who gets severe headaches from sugar, yet she won't give up her sweetened tea!) Sugar is addictive. There are antioxidants in tea that are good for us, so why drink the sodas that cost much more and are harmful besides? You're careful what kind of gas and oil you put in your car or truck, so why not be just as careful about what you put in your body? And it's much more important, because we can buy a new car or truck if it quits!

An achievement today is _____

_____

_____

_____

_____

_____

_____

_____

AUGUST 19

It is like a man away on a journey...
– Mark 13: 34

If you've been good about walking every day, and you've been walking for an hour, you can be proud of yourself. And you're doing a tremendous service to your mind and body. If you've been walking just fifteen minutes, then keep expanding the length of time until you're up to an hour (or more.) It's helpful to keep track of your efforts in your journal. Using the code W for walking works for me. Some days I can't put a W in my journal. Maybe it started raining, or I was delayed in town and didn't get back until dark. I don't walk in the dark. If you keep track of your exercise, whatever it is, use a code that works for you. This easy method helps motivate us because it elevates our mood as we watch the journal entries stack up.

An achievement today is_____

_____

_____

_____

_____

_____

_____

AUGUST 20

...was lost and has been found.

– Luke 15: 32

When I'm feeling downhearted, I ask God to send me an encouraging sign. One day recently I was feeling dreadful because one of the people that means the most to me was going through a frightening, life-threatening experience, and was told he had only weeks to live because of it. My heart was breaking, and felt heavy as concrete. I was sitting outside my farmhouse in the sunshine, when a truck pulled up and a young man jumped out. He was trying to sell me some roofing paint to cover my metal roof. I told him that I wasn't interested, but he kept pressing on and on. I finally told him, with tears in my eyes, that I was going through a terrible time, and he threw his arms around me, and said he'd pray for me and my friend. Then, right after he left, at *least* one thousand blackbirds descended on the two trees just twenty feet to the right of me. They chattered and carried on for a good fifteen minutes before flying off in a great black cloud. And I did feel so encouraged by all my visitors that day.

A sign for me today is_____

_____

AUGUST 21

And after the sun had risen, it was scorched; and because it had no root, it withered away.

– Mark 4: 6

Virginia Satir, a famous psychologist, drew a simple diagram to illustrate what happens when we're making a big life change, such as relocating. We start out with a burst of enthusiasm, then somewhere in the middle of the process, we decide the whole thing is turning out to be way too difficult, and we want to give up and go back to where we started. It's at this point, that we need some encouragement from the other end, the finish line. Maybe a friend beckoning to us, maybe a job we want there, or something else that is enticing us. The important thing is to find support for what it is we want to do that will help us carry out the process of change, and achieve our aim. Another big reason for working our support system.

An achievement today is_____
_____
_____
_____
_____
_____

AUGUST 22

For what will a man give in exchange for his soul?
– Mark 8: 37

You may have heard it said, "If God didn't make it, don't eat it." This referring to foods available today that are so processed and full of preservatives, food coloring, and additives that they barely resemble food anymore. Eating such foods may create "brain fog" or just plain fuzzy thinking. The more we take the time to prepare food 'from scratch' at home, the better off we'll be, mentally and physically. Keep eating out to a minimum, if you can. Avoid fast food, sugar and sodas and see if your thinking seems clearer. I know when I eat wild greens such as dandelion, I feel energized and much healthier, and my vision improves as well. And when I pick greens in my yard, I know they are pesticide free.

An achievement today is_____
_____
_____
_____
_____
_____
_____

AUGUST 23

...And do you not remember...

– Mark 8: 18

Congratulations if you've been keeping a dream journal. If not, think about doing this, even if you can only remember snatches of your dreams. The more often you faithfully record whatever it is you do recall, the more you will remember. It's about honoring your dreams. It is so important to pay attention to our dreams. There was an incredible event in a small town in Alabama that I read about in the Birmingham newspaper a few years ago. A man reported that a murdered woman from his town appeared to him in his dream and named her husband as the murderer. Because of this dream, the police reopened the old case and discovered new evidence that the woman's husband was indeed her murderer!

An important dream I've had is_____

_____

_____

_____

_____

_____

_____

AUGUST 24

...you have become well; do not sin any more, so that nothing worse happens to you.

– John 5: 14

If you or someone you know has been struggling with a harmful addiction, consider this interesting, effective concept by Gary Zukov as described in his book, *The Seat of the Soul*. He talks about not fearing the urge to engage in the addictive activity again, but to see any urges to drink, smoke, use, gamble, etc. as a new challenge. An urge to once again engage in the destructive activity gives us a chance to demonstrate that our whole new way of being is *stronger* than the addiction! He goes on to say that the individual typically fears those compelling urges to use because he/she mistakenly thinks that the addiction is stronger than they are. Each time they prove still again that *they* are stronger, makes them even that much more stronger!

I demonstrated strength today by_____

_____

_____

_____

_____

_____

AUGUST 25

Did not Moses give you the Law, and yet none of you carries out the Law...

– John 7: 19

If you've noticed a trace of bitterness owing to some past wrong against you, pray that God will help you overcome this. (You can read what St. Paul has to say about the root of bitterness in Hebrews 12:15.) We don't want bitterness to send out roots and cause even more trouble than has already taken place. This doesn't just affect our moods, it affects others that come into our presence as well. They can feel that vibration of bitterness even if they're not aware of it. It's not healthy for our physical or mental health. Expressing any resentments, anger, or related feelings in our journal is helpful. Talking to someone about it is helpful. And transforming it into the energy to create something new is pure alchemy! This results in an expanded feeling, rather than the constricted, unhealthy feeling of bitterness.

An achievement today is_____

_____

_____

_____

_____

AUGUST 26

...are you angry with Me because I made an entire man well on the Sabbath?

–John 7: 23

A longtime friend of mine was going through a frustrating period owing to an injury that prevented her from her daily routine of walking five miles. (An example of withdrawal from a positive addiction.) During that unwelcome down time, she began to investigate her family background. She discovered that her great, great grandfather came to this country from England as a preacher. He was one of John Wesley's most devoted followers who had come here to bring Methodism to America. This led to more research and study, which did a great deal to improve my friend Anne's mood during her recuperation. She even resumed going to church, something she hadn't gotten around to doing for a long while.

Something I'd like to learn more about is_____

_____

_____

_____

_____

_____

AUGUST 27

…You cannot make the attendants of the bridegroom fast…

– Luke 5: 34

In the book of Daniel, we learn that Daniel asked to be given vegetables and water rather than the rich food and wine of King Nebuchadnezzar's table. Despite the fears of the chief chamberlain that the men wouldn't do well on such a diet, Daniel and his friends looked better and healthier than the men who ate at the king's table. It may seem simplistic to say that eating more vegetables and drinking more water will stabilize and improve our mood, but nevertheless, this will have good effect on our mental and physical well being. When we let the healthy part of our personality make plans for us, this leads to even more health. When we let the addictive part of our personality out, however, we're setting ourselves up for more unhealthy behavior. And junk food can be so addictive. I don't buy it cause I know I'll whip right through it!

An achievement today is_____
_____
_____
_____
_____

AUGUST 28

Why do you call Me, 'Lord, Lord,' and do not do what I say?

– Luke 6: 46

In the Oxford Dictionary, we learn the etymology of the word 'resentment' means hearing the same thing over and over. If we recognize we are hurt or injured by someone's remark or action, and we deal with it as best we can...then to repeat it over and over to ourselves, like a run-on cassette tape, is counter-productive and harmful to our mental and physical health. If we become aware that we are reliving past painful or hurtful events over and over, we need to interrupt the movie. We may be doing it because we're tired, hungry, or bored, or avoiding something we need to be doing. If you're chewing over some past hurt that you're sick and tired of hearing still again, interrupt the thoughts and go outside for a brisk walk, or pursue some other activity to interrupt that boring tape.

A past hurt I'm tired of replaying is_____

_____

_____

_____

_____

AUGUST 29

...Do you see anything?

– Mark 8: 23

Another reason to pay attention to our dreams is because sometimes our dreams will tell us something we need to be eating or drinking. For example, I've dreamed that I needed to eat some beets, and on another occasion, carrots. I've dreamed of glasses of clear, pure water. If you do dream of some food your body craves, be sure to follow up. On the other hand, sometimes an alcoholic working on sobriety will dream he/she is taking a drink. This can have an upsetting effect on some people – easily remedied by getting to a meeting.

An achievement today is_____

_____

_____

_____

_____

_____

_____

_____

_____

_____

AUGUST 30

…your faith has made you well; go in peace.

– Luke 8: 48

When tuning a stringed instrument, the other strings will vibrate and resonate to the string you just tuned. You place your hand over them to stop the vibration before going on to tune the next string in line. If you let them keep resonating, it will throw your tuning off. Like the strings on a guitar, we also resonate to the sounds around us. Allow birdsong, cicadas, crickets and other nature sounds to resonate within. Our cells have to resonate enough to jarring, discordant sounds such as booming car radios, airplanes, chain saws, heavy equipment and sirens. So when we have the opportunity to resonate to pleasing sounds, it's good to remember to feel the pleasure and balancing of this. Resonating to nature helps us to stay in tune. Resonating to man made noise helps us to get out of tune with subsequent irritability and headaches.

Pleasing sounds I resonated to today are_____

_____

_____

_____

_____

AUGUST 31

...I am not strong enough to dig; I am ashamed to beg.

– Luke 16: 3

The other day Jeff and I were driving out of town and passed a motorcycle club, out in great numbers, on a poker run to raise money for a charity. We then passed a group of people in racing clothes bicycling swiftly down a country road. It gave me pleasure to see these groups of people out on such a sunny day enjoying the camaraderie and exercise of their shared interests. If there's an organization that fits your enthusiasm for something, give it a try. There are bird watching groups, canoe and hiking groups, and of course, a great many groups that get together to play different games. And if none of these interests you, perhaps there's someone nearby who would like to walk with you each day. It helps with those days when we might need a bit of encouragement to get going.

An activity I am interested in is_____

_____

_____

_____

_____

_____

SEPTEMBER 1

...Why are you reasoning in your hearts?

– Luke 5: 22

A famous writer and psychoanalyst, Clarissa Pinkola Estes, assures us that stories are medicine. If there is a story or book that is of interest to you, see about getting started on it and into it. There are thousands of wonderful tales we can pick up at the library or used book stores. Stories that chronicle adventures, challenges, risks and discoveries of people going back thousands of years. As we enter into the world a good writer has created for us, we go into a kind of revitalizing trance state. Getting into a gripping story gives us a break from whatever it is we've been going through. And often we can gain courage and insights from these stories as we follow the protagonist through his/her struggles.

A favorite story of mine is_____

_____

_____

_____

_____

_____

_____

_____

SEPTEMBER 2

The one who listens to you listens to Me...

– Luke 10: 16

Dr. Larry Dossey, in *Healing Words*, gives specific examples of what he calls *nonlocal thought* or distance thinking. If there is someone you know who is ill or hurting, you can send thoughts of comfort and healing to them. The way I do this is to picture the person I'm sending to, and visualize them surrounded by sparkling iridescent light. I stay with the visualization for as long as I feel the need to. I picture the shimmering light moving all around them, blanketing them in this warm cloud of protection. It's good to write down the date and time that you do this. Sometimes you may find out later the person felt this warm comfort at the same time you were sending it!

An achievement today is_____

_____
_____
_____
_____
_____
_____

SEPTEMBER 3

...your faith has made you well...

– Mark 5: 34

If we feel forlorn and forgotten, we would do well to remember that God has much more in store for us than we can imagine in a depressed state of mind. Remember if we're depressed, we're not tuning in to God's channel. If we use our internal tuner, we can change the dial from a dismal station, to the higher frequency of God's channel. And we *always have that choice!* No matter how downhearted or sad we may be, we can always change that dial. How do we know we're on God's channel? We feel that humming radiance, something like the purring of a cat, throughout our body. That's our natural state. We're meant to feel joyful and happy to be alive.

An achievement today is_____

_____

_____

_____

_____

_____

_____

_____

SEPTEMBER 4

For everyone who exalts himself will be humbled, and he who humbles himself will be exalted.

– Luke 14: 11

On Yom Kippur, or the Day of Atonement, Jews say prayers of penitence for anything they've done wrong during the past year, are forgiven for their mistakes, and are cleansed of these as they say goodbye to the year past. This comes soon after Rosh Hashanah has signaled the new year of the Jewish calendar, and is a reminder for us to start fresh. This tells us we no longer have to lug around baggage from the past. If we repent of our mistakes and pray for forgiveness, we *are* forgiven.

Put the suitcases full of guilt and recriminations down and walk away. This frees all that energy we tie up when we drag around all that dead weight from the past.

A mistake I forgive myself for and let go of is _____

_____

_____

_____

_____

_____

_____

SEPTEMBER 5

And I, if I am lifted up from the earth, will draw all men to Myself.

– John 12: 32

I've learned a lot from my roosters. They stand tall *all* the time. They strut around the yard and the fields, and stay always so alert as they watch for danger while the hens are poking about scratching for grubs and worms. I love to admire their glossy, bright colors, along with the grand flourish of their brilliant curved tail feathers. If a rooster becomes injured for some reason, he may retreat to a hiding place to recuperate, but he'll emerge as soon as possible into the barnyard, all flamboyant and full of spirit and determination once more. I stand straighter whenever I see a rooster strutting around the barnyard. Their spirit rubs off on me!

An achievement today is_____

_____

_____

_____

_____

_____

_____

_____

SEPTEMBER 6

I know Him, because I am from Him, and He sent Me.

–John 7: 29

Euclid was a proponent of learning for its own sake, and not only because it's "practical." There are many people who won't spend time to learn something, unless they can "use" the information. If there's something that interests you, yet you can't see how you'll "use" the knowledge, study it anyway. It's good brain exercise, and if it's a subject we enjoy, the learning will be of great benefit to us in terms of a sense of well-being. And if it's a subject you don't know much about yet, a book about it for young adults is an easy way to check it out. Learning a little about something can lead to wanting to learn even more. And this is still another way of getting away from any gloomy, self-defeating thoughts we may have been having.

A topic that interests me is_____

_____

_____

_____

_____

_____

_____

SEPTEMBER 7

Consider the ravens, for they neither sow nor reap; they have no storehouse nor barn, and yet God feeds them...

– Luke 12: 24

So much of Jesus' parables use agricultural language. Harvests, sowing seeds, fields, soil farm work, open skies, stones, all figure in his teachings. I am so grateful to be able to look out at fields and woods all around the farmhouse. The tall native grass in the fields is a reddish gold and bends with the wind. A multitude of trees surrounds the fields. One of the reasons I love to read the gospels is all these pastoral scenes that I can see so vividly in my mind. So many millions of people live surrounded by concrete and buildings, removed from the country. If you are in a city and can somehow get out of there to the country, the change can be transforming. If you can't get out of the city right now, then go to the country in your mind.

An achievement today is_____

_____

_____

_____

_____

_____

SEPTEMBER 8

...do not rejoice in this, that the spirits are subject to you, but rejoice that your names are recorded in heaven.

– Luke 10: 20

Sometimes when listening to the radio, a station can slip in and out, so that we have to adjust the tuner to get reception back clearly again. If we find we are slipping out of tune, we need to readjust our internal tuner and get back on a frequency that feels right to us. When we're on a good frequency, things in our life go smoothly. When we're out of tune, things will break or go wrong, accidents will often happen, and we may end up drained, frustrated, and weary. The other day I was experiencing a great deal of tension owing to some unforeseen events. I believe it was because of this tension that three very unusual and frustrating things happened which interrupted me from going about my daily farm chores. That is until I realized that I was completely out of tune, and my frequency badly needed a rapid adjustment.

An achievement today is_____

_____

_____

_____

SEPTEMBER 9

...I am the Light of the world; he who follows Me will not walk in the darkness, but will have the Light of life.

−John 8: 12

Jesus loved the outcasts, the marginal people, the outsiders, and the socially unacceptable. He spent time with the people we refer to today as street people. And he was highly criticized for this by the "respectable" people who were watching him carefully. If you feel you are viewed as a misfit or an outsider, consider what we have learned from Jesus about those who look down upon others. And if you have ever looked upon others as marginal and not worth your time, you might want to reconsider that point of view. They may be much more "in tune" than you think or believe. •

A "fringe" person I know is_____

_____

_____

_____

_____

_____

_____

_____

SEPTEMBER 10

...Stop! No more of this...
– Luke 22: 51

If you are retired or not working for some other reason, don't fall into the trap of thinking that day after day of recreation and amusements is good for you. Having lived in a Florida resort for many years, I saw wide spread evidence of this. Meaningful work is critically important to every individual's healthy brain function. It's fine and dandy to play golf or tennis every day, or to pursue other self-comforting amusements, but for optimal brain function, we need to involve ourselves in work that we personally see as meaningful. What is meaningful to one individual is different than what is meaningful to another. Maybe one person's work is in mentoring or tutoring. Another's may be in playing with the local symphony, or getting out a newsletter. There is a group of retired detectives in Little Rock that have been very successful in opening up and solving cold cases. In just amusing ourselves, we run the risk of putting our brain out to pasture, which can turn it to mush in a hurry!

Meaningful work to me would be_____

_____

_____

SEPTEMBER 11

...lift up your eyes and look on the fields, that they are white for harvest.

–John 4: 35

Growing plants improves mood. You can root plants in water and watch them grow on your windowsill. You can plant easy vegetables among the flowers in your garden. You can cut the green tops off scallions and plant the bottom white part in soil so that you will have green onion tops replenishing all the time. All you have to do is snip off the top inches for your soups and salads. (Same is true for garlic, and garlic greens add great flavor to soups and stews.) The more plants you grow in your environment, the more tranquil will be your living space and the fresher the air. If you are short on space, perhaps living in an apartment, do what the crowded Japanese do. Container gardens! They are world champions of the container garden, and grow an incredible amount of vegetables in pots. Start with easy ones at first.

A favorite vegetable I'd like to grow_____
_____
_____
_____

SEPTEMBER 12

And He will send forth His angels with a great trumpet...
– Matthew 24: 31

If you've ever tried to play a violin, then you know you have to find the notes. There are no frets as in a guitar to help you. Some days we may awaken in a dismal mood and have to "find the notes" that will make it a better day. In other words we have to *make* our day. We have to build our day from the bottom up. If I want to reset my mood in the morning, I listen to music to which I resonate. Music that will create a different internal environment for me. We have musical memory, and we can use it to our advantage by listening to music we love over and over until it reprograms our inner space. I even wrote a song about this called *The Jukebox in My Mind.*

Music that improves my mood is_____

_____
_____
_____
_____
_____
_____
_____

SEPTEMBER 13

But they do all their deeds to be noticed by men...

– Matthew 23: 5

Is there a part of your personality that you never let out because it doesn't have a "practical" or money-making potential? Maybe you are a closet actor, or dancer, or poet or song writer. And the chances of turning that talent into a paycheck were so slim that you never gave it expression. If, however, you do give just an hour or two a day to some expression of a forgotten and ignored part of your personality, you may find a rush of energy that is unleashed as you take that part out of storage and dust it off. Along with the energy, you may find you feel a renewed sense of well being...all this because of rounding out your personality a bit more. And actualizing an important part of you that has been labeled unimportant in the past, by you or someone in your environment. Definitely worth pondering.

A part of me that I have ignored is_____

_____

_____

_____

_____

SEPTEMBER 14

...See to it that no one misleads you.

– Matthew 24: 4

Did you know William Tyndale was burned at the stake just for translating the Bible into English? Henry VIII was furious with him for daring to pursue such an outlawed act! Tyndale was a brilliant scholar and studied many languages. He translated the New Testament from the Greek, and then learned Hebrew so he could translate the Old Testament. But his work was interrupted by an evil plan to find him in Europe and execute him. A friend/traitor was able to bring this about. Many innocent people were also executed just for having Tyndale's Bible in their possession, or just for being his friend. So when reading your Bible, be grateful to the martyrs that helped bring Scripture to you in such an accessible form. It wasn't always so.

My favorite Bible story is_____

_____

_____

_____

_____

_____

_____

SEPTEMBER 15

*He was the lamp that was burning and was shining and
you were willing to rejoice for a while in his light.*

–John 5: 35

It's one thing to stay inside on cold, dark, rainy days,
but when the sun is out, get outside! We aren't designed
to be cooped up inside in the dark, like bears hibernat-
ing in a cave. We need fresh air and sunlight. We need
to hear the healing sounds of nature. With the advent
of computers and the Internet, more and more people
are sitting like robots in front of that screen, plugged
into the Internet, for hours and hours, breathing
canned air, when they could be outside inhaling fresh
air and light. As Americans grow more and more sedentary, and further and further away from our adven-
turous, frontier roots, we are distancing ourselves from
even what it means to be human, because of a growing
isolation. We are mammals, and need interaction with
the rest of nature for optimal health and well-being.

Activities I did outdoors today were_____
_____
_____
_____
_____

SEPTEMBER 16

…You deaf and mute spirit, I command you, come out of him and do not enter him again.

– Mark 9: 25

Once we've learned to manage our thoughts so that they don't steer us into uncomfortable emotions, we feel such relief that we are no longer stewing in those juices that once held us captive. (They didn't really hold us captive, we just believed they did!) Allowing unwanted thoughts to spin around in our mind is like turning on a slow cooker and letting it simmer all day. But when we've learned the secret of unplugging the slow cooker, we are free to enjoy the day, despite whatever it is we're going through.

Remember to look for and expect a surprise from God every day. The other day my surprise was a blue egg! One of my chickens laid a beautiful pale blue egg, and I don't understand how, because she isn't an Auracola hen.

An achievement today is_____

_____

_____

_____

_____

SEPTEMBER 17

…Take this and share it among yourselves.

– Luke 22: 17

If you or someone you care about is struggling with bipolar disorder, you may be interested in reading Patty Duke's book about her experiences with this. Another good book is *An Unquiet Mind* by Kay Jamison, a psychiatrist who writes about how she learned to manage her own difficulties with this disorder. When it comes to chemical imbalances, modern medicine has progressed enough that individuals can maintain successful lives and function well despite the cards they were dealt. Information is important. And there's plenty of information on the subject out there.

An achievement today is_____

_____

_____

_____

_____

_____

_____

_____

_____

SEPTEMBER 18

Go; behold, I send you out as lambs in the midst of wolves.

– Luke 10: 3

Jesus taught us to love one another, and He also taught caution when dealing with others. He was sending the disciples out to preach, teach, and heal. And He didn't want them to spend time with people who were not welcoming or receptive to their message. If you interact with people, and work to encourage them, follow Jesus' advice and leave if you are not welcomed, or feel disrespected in any way. However, when you interact with receptive people, the light you send out will shine right back at you.

An achievement today is _____

_____

_____

_____

_____

_____

_____

_____

_____

SEPTEMBER 19

...Yes, Father, for this way was well-pleasing in Your sight..
– Luke 10: 21

You've heard the quote: "We are spiritual beings living in a physical body." When we forget this, and get out of balance and are obsessing over worldly concerns, we may suffer from a disturbed mood. However, by reestablishing a connection to our spiritual self, we get back into balance and right ourselves emotionally. Maintaining a daily practice of study, contemplation, and prayer helps keep us in balance, so that if something upsets us, we are not shaken from our spiritual connection. Turning to spiritual study, prayer and contemplation only when something has shaken us up takes a while longer to calm us, because we have allowed ourselves to become too much caught up in the snares of the world.

An achievement today is_____

_____

_____

_____

_____

_____

_____

SEPTEMBER 20

Again, the kingdom of heaven is like a merchant seeking fine pearls...

– Matthew 13: 45

We cherish those times when we feel the bliss of being in tune with God. And getting back to that state of being is like that merchant searching for fine pearls. All of Jesus' teachings are trying to guide us to that blissful, heavenly state – when we are so in tune that we are positively humming inside. When we are in tune, our day goes smoothly, our body/mind is working with top efficiency, and we are glowing. If we're feeling lousy, we can remind ourselves that we are out of tune and we need to tune up. There are many ways of doing this, but we know we must first interrupt whatever circular thinking is going on in our head. Remember, allowing disturbing thoughts to continue on that mental merry-go-round assures only more dismal feelings. Interrupt all that *stinking thinking* how you so choose. But do interrupt that relentless cycle, and go hunting for fine pearls instead.

An achievement today is_____

_____

_____

_____

SEPTEMBER 21

Take My yoke upon you and learn from Me, for I am gentle and humble in heart, and you will find rest for your souls.

– Matthew 11: 29

There's an old saying that all we can take to our grave is what we've managed to give away. An old Alabama farm woman friend told me she believes in going through life with open hands, because when we hang onto things, our hands are tightly closed. Sometimes, if going through a time of despondency, we may well need to let go of some things, (or people), to break up the density of mood disorder. In our consumer oriented society, most of us are encumbered and weighed down with unnecessary things. Selling them or giving them away can be truly mood elevating.

Something I can give away today is_____

_____

_____

_____

_____

_____

_____

_____

SEPTEMBER 22

*...I am the bread of life; he who comes to Me will not hunger,
and he who believes in Me will never thirst.*

– John 6: 35

A good movie with the theme of finding what you really want to do, and doing it, despite society's way of looking at things is: *Tenure,* with Luke Wilson. What our culture perceives as a successful career is not necessarily the same as what an individual really wants. It can often be hard for an individual to discover where his/her heart really lies given the pressures of family and the larger group. Some years ago, when I was torn about moving to where I wanted to be, which is one thousand miles and three states to the west of my family, my friend Mary said, "Do what you want...cause you know your family is sure going to do whatever they want!" And, did she ever have that right!

An achievement today is_____

_____

_____

_____

_____

_____

SEPTEMBER 23

...Go, wash in the Pool of Siloam...
– John 9: 7

A hot bath with all the accessories can disarm and interrupt a low mood. If you light candles and use bubble bath or bath oils or otherwise make a production out of it, you can turn an everyday bath into an experience that will transform a dismal mood. The combination of aromas from the soap, the bath oils and the gentle wavering light of the candles and the heat of the bath water all combine to soothe and relax a troubled spirit. After a brisk rub down with a towel, we feel quite differently than when we stepped into the tub.

An achievement today is_____

_____

_____

_____

_____

_____

_____

_____

_____

_____

SEPTEMBER 24

...Does this cause you to stumble?

– John 6: 61

If you've been through a traumatic experience, and you are suffering in the aftermath of this, remember to be kind to yourself and allow plenty of time for rest and recuperation from the event. Whether it's a death of a person you love, or a pet, or a car accident, or some other tragic event, you need to allow yourself time to recover from the shock of this to your nervous system. You might have to show up at work the next day, but when you get home, treat yourself with special, tender care. And continue to do so for as long as you need to. (Lavender oil helps relieve agitation).

An achievement today is_____

_____

_____

_____

_____

_____

_____

_____

SEPTEMBER 25

...Get up and come forward!

– Mark 3: 3

Jesus called to the man with the withered hand. Do you ever picture yourself in some of those long ago Bible scenes? Can you imagine what it was like back then, so you can be one of the crowd watching and listening as Jesus spoke? One of the dreams that I cherish from a few years ago was this: I was standing with a crowd on the bank of a river, and Jesus was baptizing someone. I was quite near to Him, and I still have a clear memory of that vivid dream, even to the coarse weave of the clothes worn by all of us. Next time you read a chapter from the Gospels, imagine yourself right there in the midst of the story.

One of my favorite Gospel stories is_____

_____

_____

_____

_____

_____

_____

_____

_____

SEPTEMBER 26

...because they repented at the preaching of Jonah; and behold, something greater than Jonah is here.

– Matthew 12: 41

Jonah ran from God's assignment, but in the end he did what he was supposed to do, and preached at Nineveh. Is there something that perhaps you feel called upon to do by God that you've neglected to pursue? If so, see about doing a little bit toward this each day. Remember, working by increments is the magic key to accomplishing those tasks we keep putting off because they seem to be overwhelming. And even if we only do a little bit, we will experience improved mood each small step of the way.

An achievement today is_____

_____

_____

_____

_____

_____

_____

_____

_____

SEPTEMBER 27

…and came to him and bandaged up his wounds…

– Luke 10: 34

If we experience a period of reactive depression because of something that has wounded us, we can treat the wounds through therapy, support groups, and other therapeutic methods. If we know someone who has been wounded, we can, like the Good Samaritan Jesus refers to in the above verse, come to their aid as well. And we can be assured that helping another is *always* going to elevate our mood. I saw a pickup slide down the boat ramp into the Bayou Teche as a man was putting his boat into the water. Within five minutes three pickups had stopped, and the drivers were running with chains to pull the man's truck out of the water. (This is just another example I've witnessed of Cajuns reacting swiftly in an emergency to help others. You should have seen them rescuing people, horses, and cattle during Hurricane Rita.)

An achievement today is _____

_____

_____

_____

_____

SEPTEMBER 28

Whoever then humbles himself as this child, he is the greatest in the kingdom of heaven.

– Matthew 18: 4

Our ego gets us into trouble with regularity. If our feelings are hurt, wounded, offended, etc., we can be certain our ego is involved in the mix. Most bouts of depression are made up of a stew of conflicting emotions and you can be sure the ego is right in there, twisting and turning! Recognizing this is helpful, because our self coaching can include a reminder that the ego is causing a good deal of our emotional discomfort. We don't have to put up with the demands of our ego. We can practice humility instead and talk back to our ego once in a while! Back off, ego! Lighten up!

An achievement today is _____

_____

_____

_____

_____

_____

_____

_____

SEPTEMBER 29

...Are there not twelve hours in the day? If anyone walks in the day, he does not stumble, because he sees the light of this world.

–John 11: 9

When experiencing a dreary mood, we need to get out into the sunlight. And metaphorically, the interior darkness that can go along with a depressed mood can be chased away by shining our light within. And our inner light is always shining, despite the shadows that may obscure it from time to time. When we are in a dark mood, we may "stumble," because we are not seeing clearly. By increasing the light within, by acts of kindness, bravery, and generosity of spirit, we banish those internal shadows, one by gloomy one.

An achievement today is _____

_____

_____

_____

_____

_____

_____

_____

SEPTEMBER 30

...I who speak to you am He.

−John 4: 26

There is a young boy whose mother went to a halfway house for addictions. She had lost custody of him, and so he went to live with his grandmother. He felt so lost and lonely, he put a little snail (without the shell) into his ear, but didn't tell anyone about it. The snail dug in and wrapped itself around his cochlear nerve, and had to be surgically removed. The young boy finally spoke about it, explaining that the snail was his friend and talked to him. He was so lonely, he needed to create a friendship with a snail! This sad story is true, and reveals to what extremes a lonely individual may go. So, if you know someone who is lonely, you might give them a call or pay a visit.

An achievement today is_____
_____
_____
_____
_____
_____
_____
_____

OCTOBER 1

...The kingdom of heaven may be compared to a man who sowed good seed in his field.

– Matthew 13: 24

Autumn brings brilliant colors along with the season. Those deep reds, the gold, the burnt orange, the bright yellow, all combine to make a startlingly beautiful landscape. One good visualization to remember is to watch an autumn leaf slowly drifting with the current of a stream or a creek. And as you watch the leaf gently bobbing as it floats along, smell the crisp air of autumn, and feel the coolness of it on your skin. Then be sure to take notice of the tension in your body melting away as the leaf drifts along on the water. You may even notice a tingling in your body as your muscles relax, and this relief from tension is so welcome, so restful.

A restful image for me is_____
_____
_____
_____
_____
_____
_____

OCTOBER 2

...for they say things and do not do them.

– Matthew 23: 3

Jesus didn't come to start a religion. He spoke out against legalism and the many rules and regulations of formal religion. What he taught instead is, how we can have a direct communication with God. He taught us to talk to God directly in prayer, and to do it often during the day. As far as the rules and regulations, He taught us to use common sense in regard to these. Such legalisms as how to keep the Sabbath, and dietary laws didn't mean as much to Jesus as using common sense depending on the circumstances, and loving our neighbor.

An achievement today is_____
_____
_____
_____
_____
_____
_____
_____
_____
_____

OCTOBER 3

...For behold, the Kingdom of God is in your midst.

– Luke 17: 21

All Souls' Day, which is also called Halloween, is a day for costumes for both children and often, adults as well. If you were interested in dressing up in a costume, what or who might you choose to look like? Let your imagination go, without judgment, and see what pops into your head. This experiment might reveal to you a piece of your personality that you have not recognized or allowed "out." It's interesting to me that the Pirate costume has been so frequently used by adults. This suggests to me that people are hungry for adventure, because they so often seek safe, comfortable lives, with as little risk taken as possible. This also explains the huge popularity that adventure/action movies have had in our culture. It's a safe way to indulge in risky pursuits without the danger.

A costume that appeals to me is_____

_____

_____

_____

_____

_____

OCTOBER 4

…What do you seek?…

–John 1: 38

Some of my chickens are called Frizzle Cochins. They have curly feathers and are very handsome. I delight in looking at my roosters and chickens, and most especially delight in admiring my Frizzles. (I never eat them, but I do love hunting their eggs.) Their glossy feathers look like they're wind-blown. Trying to protect my hens from predators while they're setting on their eggs, and after the eggs have hatched helping to keep them safe is a job. If we're lucky, and the chicks manage to grow big enough to fly up into the trees so as to be safe at night, the hardest part is over. Wherever our interests lie, it is so important to our vitality and sense of well being to pursue those interests. And if those interests benefit other living creatures, that's even better. (Isn't it interesting that a hen setting on her eggs in a dark hidden place is called a broody hen? And we refer to someone staying in the house alone, hidden from the outside world, as brooding.) Just saying!

An interest of mine is_____
_____
_____
_____

OCTOBER 5

...A lamp is not brought to be put under a basket, is it, or under a bed? Is it not brought to be put on the lampstand?

– Mark 4: 21

Be aware of every time you expand, and shine your light outward. Also, be aware of every time you contract or shut down and keep your light hidden. When we are generous, kind, considerate, thoughtful, or giving, we are expanding and shining our light. Those times we are holding back, grasping, sarcastic, condescending, or out and out rude, we are contracting and obscuring our light. When we expand, we feel good. When we contract, we feel out of sorts, out of tune, and are feeding the Dismal Swamp of thoughts. It's like the food that gets shoved to the back of the refrigerator. It turns into science experiments and grows mold on its surfaces. And that's what happens when we stay contracted, obscuring our light. We too can grow moldy and fuzzy thoughts!

An achievement today is_____

_____

_____

_____

_____

OCTOBER 6

...love your enemies and pray for those who persecute you.

– Matthew 5: 44

By forgiving others, we acknowledge that we're not saints either. And we also acknowledge that we don't know what circumstances have combined to make the individual in question do something hurtful or harmful. Only God knows what twists people into harmful attitudes and world views. However, to forgive doesn't mean we have to be Polyannas, or naïve, and set ourselves up for more hurt. Forgiving is one thing, and allowing ourselves to be further manipulated or disrespected or cheated or whatever it was that caused the emotional damage is another. Discernment is a good thing. So release the resentment, and be more cautious the next time.

An achievement today is_____
_____
_____
_____
_____
_____
_____
_____

OCTOBER 7

From the days of John the Baptist until now the kingdom of heaven suffers violence, and violent men take it by force.

– Matthew 11: 12

If you've ever studied Chaos Theory, then you know that this refers to the unpredictability of some aspects of the Universe. While much of the Universe adheres to strict laws, and is predictable, some parts of it do not. Well, certainly we can believe this, because as a microcosm of the Universe, our moods and thoughts are not predictable all the time, by any means. So Chaos Theory is a concept that is not so difficult to understand in our own life…. and in that of those around us. Scientists include the weather in the Chaos Theory. No surprise there! And we can make plans for times we know can be difficult for us. Some people get blue on rainy or overcast days. Some people hurt on chilly or cold days because of old bone breaks, arthritis, or other problems. As mentioned earlier in another entry, twilight can be a hard time for some people, and early mornings for some others. The more we learn to work with our moods, instead of feeling victimized by them, we better we are going to feel.

Weather that negatively affects my mood is_____

OCTOBER 8

But no one can enter the strong man's house and plunder his property unless he first binds the strong man...

– Mark 3: 27

Delbert McClinton sings a song titled, *I'm a Victim of Life's Circumstances.* Sometimes people are victims of a crime, or unfair treatment that doesn't quite qualify as a crime. However, it's good to analyze what has victimized us, and how we can avoid this happening to us again. As they say, live and learn. Taking precautions such as always locking your doors and not wandering around by yourself at night, sometimes aren't enough to avoid trouble, but at least we're reducing the risk. A real danger though is to adopt a victim persona, and self label as: Victim. In doing so, we keep drawing that energy to ourselves. Some people repeatedly recount past experiences in which they were victimized, and don't seem to grow weary of reviewing these old hurts. A reminder: Visualize a mist or heavy fog falling all over any past painful experiences you find yourself revisiting. Let the mist obscure the memory and set you free of it.

An achievement today is_____

_____

_____

OCTOBER 9

At the harvest time...

– Mark 12: 2

Often, in the country, people put autumn displays in their front yard. This might consist of a stack of pumpkins on a hay bale with a scarecrow dangled on a pole, or a red wagon filled with pumpkins and potted gold and orange chrysanthemums. This simple display is fun to see when you're driving out in the country, and it's easy to do, even if you're in town. If you don't have a front yard, consider making a wreath of twigs, autumn leaves, and acorns for your front door. Or just set a pumpkin by the threshold. And, when getting ready to scrape out the pumpkin, be sure to save those seeds. They're loaded with vitamins and minerals, and when lightly salted and toasted in the oven, they are delicious.

An achievement today is_____

_____

_____

_____

_____

_____

_____

OCTOBER 10

...Ephphatha!... Be opened...
– Mark 7: 34

Kathleen Norris in her book, "The Cloister Walk," speaks of the two to three beat count that is built into Gregorian Chants, and how this has been interpreted as a good rhythm for our brains. This rhythm leads to a sense of well-being. As we resonate to sounds that feel good, we are accelerating healing, both of mind and body. Many cultures have healing chants, and ancient people were well aware of the beneficial results of those sounds. The ancient healing ragas of India were said to cause our cells to get back into balance because of the tones in the singing. The theory is that disease causes cells to fall out of balance, but the healing sounds can correct that. Sikh friends gave me a CD of some of their sacred music. I listened to it over and over because it made me feel good, despite not understanding a word of it. So, even if you don't understand Latin, Hindu, Hebrew, or whatever language is sung, listen to recordings that make you feel good. Fortunately, You-Tube has made many of these accessible for everyone.

Some sounds that I love to hear are_____
_____

OCTOBER 11

...take away the talent from him, and give it to the one who has the ten talents.

– Matthew 25: 28

Go ahead. Make someone's day! My former husband, Buddy, likes to drop a dollar bill on the sidewalk on purpose. He says he does this because it'll make the person who finds it happy. Thinking up a way to add a bit of cheer to another's day will definitely lift your spirits as well. And these little acts of spontaneity can mean a whole lot more to the person on the receiving end. The Little Rock paper has a feature called Postcards From the Past. They print picture post cards from Arkansas that people have saved for almost a century. Such a small action to buy a postcard and drop it in the mail....and who knows, it might mean so much to the receiver, that it will be saved for decades.

An achievement today is_____

_____

_____

_____

_____

_____

_____

OCTOBER 12

But many who are first will be last; and the last, first.

– Matthew 19: 30

City people have been known to look down upon rural people, even going so far as to call them "hicks." Wannabe intellectuals have been known to look down upon or dismiss those who barely got through high school. Yet what they're missing is that everyone has expertise, but in different areas. If a catastrophe hits a big city, most of the residents who are dependent upon trucks bringing food in from the country are in trouble. If there's a blackout, they panic, whereas country people don't, because they have generators or lanterns for backup. Someone who feels superior to others, but who is lost in a storm with his car in a ditch, would be most welcoming to an uneducated man, who stopped by to give him a hand. So, if anyone has looked down upon you because you don't measure up to their standards, know that all they're doing is displaying their ignorance and personal bias – and it has nothing to do with you.

Expertise that I have is_____

_____

_____

_____

OCTOBER 13

...for there is nothing concealed that will not be revealed...
– Matthew 10: 26

Want to find something you've misplaced or lost? Finding it will elevate your mood in a hurry. So, before going to sleep, ask aloud if you could remember in a dream where you hid the object, or where you last saw it. If you've been keeping a dream journal, then you're probably remembering your dreams better than ever. So pay attention to your dreams the night that you ask for your answer, and look for your answer in subsequent dreams. You may dream in symbols and not understand the meaning at first. But if we don't "get" a dream, we will dream the information in another form on a later night, over and over, until we do understand what our dreams are telling us.

Something I'd like to find is_____
_____
_____
_____
_____
_____
_____
_____

OCTOBER 14

...Beware of the scribes who like to go around in long robes, and like respectful greetings in the market places...

– Mark 12: 38

Passive-aggressive behavior can be maddening. People who operate this way are not forthright. They do what they want, but in a backdoor, convoluted manner. For example, you ask the person to do something they don't want to do, but instead of telling you that, they do the job half-heartedly or even badly. They might not even be aware that they are doing this, because they aren't forthright with themselves either. Personally, I would prefer a person who says what's on their mind regardless. They may come off as rude to some, but they are refreshing because "what you see is what you get." They're not going to baffle you with passive-aggressive behavior because they will tell you right up front how they feel about something. It won't be a big mystery! One of the ways to lift a heavy mood is to be forthright. If you don't want to do something say so. Forget the politics of it, unless it's your boss talking, and it's part of your job.

Someone I value for speaking their mind is_____
_____
_____

OCTOBER 15

...O unbelieving generation, how long shall I be with you?
How long shall I put up with you?...

– Mark 9: 19

We're aware of animals sensing that a person doesn't like them, but we can also sense this. No matter how polite a person is, as they attempt to cover up the dislike, we can sense their dislike or disapproval. By the same token, often a gruff person likes us, and we sense this, even though their speech isn't exactly diplomatic. The more we pay attention to our "gut" feelings, the better off we'll be. Does our stomach tighten around someone? Or maybe the back of our neck? These are body signals that something isn't quite right. As we learn more and more how to rely on these body signals, we can avoid situations that may not be beneficial for us. Learning to stay alert to our body wisdom and signals will always benefit us.

A warning signal I've had is_____

_____

_____

_____

_____

OCTOBER 16

just as the Son of Man did not come to be served, but to serve...

– Matthew 20: 28

If you've ever had the opportunity to stay in the guest house of a monastery, you know that the rooms are very simply furnished. I've stayed many times in the guesthouse of a Benedictine Monastery, and enjoyed going to prayers and taking meals with the brothers and doing the chores that were assigned to me. It's a wonderful experience, and I'd recommend it to anyone. I enjoy it so much, I took my granddaughter (when she was eight) along one weekend. Ursula enjoyed herself except for the disappointment that there was no television in our room or anywhere else! If you have a convent or monastery in your area, you might ask about the possibility of staying in their guesthouse. You don't have to be a Catholic to be a guest. The fees are reasonable, and go to a good cause...that of helping the monastery or convent with their upkeep. This can be a most memorable experience, and is almost certain to provide the peace and quiet you need to receive valuable insights.

An achievement today is_____

_____

OCTOBER 17

Do not judge so that you will not be judged.

Matthew 7: 1

A beautiful song that Little Jimmy Dickens, George Jones, Conway Twitty and Ricky Van Shelton all recorded, *Life Turned Her That Way,* is a reminder that someone who is difficult or hard to understand may have gone through some severe life trials in the past. Always remember if you meet an unpleasant person that they have learned to deal with the world the hard way probably because they have been dealt some lousy cards somewhere earlier in life. A suggestion for dealing with a difficult person is to "Kill them with kindness." Often a difficult person will positively melt away when you are really, really nice to them. And by this, I don't mean in an exaggerated condescending way, for surely that will only exacerbate their attitude, but in a genuinely friendly way. Anyhow, what have you got to lose by trying it out?

A difficult person I've "melted" with kindness is_____

_____

_____

_____

_____

OCTOBER 18

An evil and unfaithful generation craves for a sign; and yet no sign will be given to it but the sign of Jonah the prophet.

– Matthew 12: 39

I live in the heart of Cajun country, and have learned from the Cajuns for decades. I raise the healing plants that the old timers used for remedies back in the day, so as to keep the traditions alive. They've also taught me many signs in nature that they use to make predictions. One of these is that when you see a large flock of blackbirds on the wing, that means cold weather is coming. Another is that winter isn't over until you see buds forming on the native pecan trees. Whatever section of the country you live in has tips from the old timers that you can research and learn from. This in itself is a most satisfying project if you are looking for something to do that will engage your interest.

And if you're learning some of these tips from elders in your area, be sure to write them down, as when the elders leave us, much of this information will go with them, unless someone has taken the time to record it.

A bit of local wisdom I like is_____
_____
_____
_____

OCTOBER 19

*… To you it has been granted to know the mysteries of the
kingdom of heaven has been granted, but to
them it has not been granted.*

– Matthew 13: 11

Music lovers are so grateful to their favorite musicians
that they frequently erect statues in their honor. We have
statues in this country of Stevie Ray Vaughn in Austin;
Jimmy Hendrix in Seattle; Ray Charles in Albany; Elvis in
Memphis; Hank Williams in Nashville; and even Johnny
Ramone in Hollywood Cemetery, (erected by Nicholas
Cage). There are many statues in honor of musicians in
Europe as well. Music is such a gift to the world, and we
have such an abundance of different kinds of music that
everyone's taste can be so easily satisfied. Maybe you down-
load music, or listen to the radio, or have a CD collection,
or make your own music, but do include music into each
day. And listen to a wide variety of styles, so as to learn how
different forms of music affect your moods. Remember the
earlier suggestion to pay as much attention to your sound
nutrition as to your food nutrition. It has a powerful sway
over our moods.

295

This is Your Brain on Music by Daniel Levitin has a wealth of information about how our brains react to music.

Music that I listened to today is_____

_____
_____
_____
_____
_____
_____

OCTOBER 20

...remain here and keep watch with Me.
– Matthew 26: 38

Remember the K.I.S.S. theory? Keep it simple, stupid! This brings a smile, but it is true. We do tend to complicate our lives much more than we need to. Whenever we think of a way to simplify our life, we're probably doing a good thing. Many of us overthink things, overdo things, and make things more difficult for ourselves than we need to. Any time we can invent an easier way of doing something, then we can feel proud. And any time we think of a way to save some time doing chores or running errands, we have that much more time available to put into achieving meaningful goals. And any progress we make toward those goals that are important to us will help to elevate our moods. Then we can bask in the pleasure of moving closer to achieving them.

Some work I did toward a goal today is_____

_____

_____

_____

_____

OCTOBER 21

So, because you are lukewarm, and neither hot nor cold, I will spit you out of My mouth.

– Revelation 3: 16

What is your passion? Whatever it is, feed it, because there lies vitality, energy, and a sense of well being. There are all sorts of passions for all sorts of people. Some are passionate about motorcycles; some about vintage cars; some about the latest technological gizmo; some about the theatre, etc. My brother has a passion for movies and owns two thousand DVDs! Enthusiasm is healthy for mind and body. What isn't healthy is to ignore our passion, and not give it any time or energy, because then we are diminishing our zest for life. Some may have a spouse who is jealous of the time spent on an enthusiasm, because they don't yet understand the importance of this. But if we are true to our authentic self, and give time and energy to nurture our passion, this will help to maintain a stable mood.

A passion that I have is_____

_____

_____

_____

OCTOBER 22

...there were many widows in Israel in the days of Elijah, when the sky was shut up for three years and six months, when a great famine came over all the land.

– Luke 4: 25

When the great prophet Elijah was depressed, he cried out to God that he wanted to die! He was despondent about the idol worship of the people. God sent an angel to visit him with food and drink, and told him to eat and drink and rest. Then he sent an angel a second time with food and drink. We can pray to God if we are feeling forlorn and despondent. And then we need to expect and stay alert for the help that is sent to us. And be aware that help may not come in any way we anticipate, but rather in a surprising, unforeseen manner.

An achievement today is_____

_____

_____

_____

_____

_____

_____

OCTOBER 23

…He himself took our infirmities and carried away our diseases.

– Matthew 8: 17

One night, during a traumatic time, I dreamed of an angel who hovered far above the Earth. He had huge gossamer wings, and I was beside him, in a blissful state, mesmerized by the iridescence of the feathers on his wings. I wanted to stay right where I was, close to him, feeling that bliss, but he said I had to go back. I cried, "Please! Let me stay with you!" but he sent me back despite the tears and begging. I've never forgotten that intense dream. It was so real! I tell you this because I believe we do have a guardian angel, and maybe more than one. And we can receive guidance from our guardian angel. But we have to stay open to this, and listen, so that we don't miss hearing any messages of guidance.

An achievement today is_____

_____

_____

_____

_____

_____

OCTOBER 24

...Watch out!...

– Mark 8: 15

Certain colors make me positively swoon. I found a fuchsia glass bottle in a junk shop, and put it on my kitchen windowsill. When I look at the glass bottle with rays of sunlight slanting through, it takes my breath away. If you read a high school Physics textbook, it will explain how color is vibration, and the result of reflected light waves. So, if we're attracted to certain colors, I believe we somehow need that form of light. Our tastes in color change from day to day, so pay attention to what colors attract your eye and please you, even mesmerize you, then try to include them in your environment to soothe and improve your mood. (You might want to avoid black and other somber low vibration colors.)

A favorite color of mine today is_____

_____

_____

_____

_____

__ _____

_____

OCTOBER 25

...Take heed, keep on the alert; for you do not know when the appointed time will come.

– Mark 13: 33

Point vierge refers to the time between daylight and darkness. If we are at that point, we are on the cusp of that dark period we may have been experiencing, and coming into the sunlight once more. We can feel the warmth of contentment rising as we look forward to the new day's efforts, and we feel the enthusiasm also rising for whatever it is we want to accomplish. Our energy, no longer bound up in self-defeating thought is released. And we can feel the confidence that comes with increased energy. The more progress we make toward our goals, the more energy becomes available. Moving through depression is a process, and the outcome of it all is that we appreciate and treasure our renewed vitality. We don't take this renewal for granted, but rather protect it by continuing to do the things that we know help us to experience an elevated mood.

An achievement today is_____

_____

_____

_____

OCTOBER 26

they will pick up serpents…
— Mark 16: 18

Recently, I walked through the woods in front of my farmhouse down the bank to the fabled Bayou Teche. I admired the muddy brown current flowing along, and then looked down. There was a water moccasin just three feet ahead of me resting on the muddy bank. Startled, I froze, then, frightened, I began slowly backing up. Moccasins have been known to go after people, so my heart was pounding, but he slipped away into the water, and that was the end of that. This story is a metaphor for temptation. Say that the snake represents temptation. If we come near to a snake, then we need to back up, turn around and go in the opposite direction. This goes for any of the addictions. Be it alcohol, drugs, gambling, wrong foods, etc. If you find yourself in the vicinity or the proximity of your addiction, then back up, turn around, and waste no time heading in the opposite direction.

A temptation for me is _____
_____
_____
_____

OCTOBER 27

...I must preach the kingdom of God to the other cities also, for I was sent for this purpose.

– Luke 4: 43

John Wesley, the founder of Methodism, used to say this grace at table. I include it here because I only recently discovered it, and found it lovely.

Be present at our table, Lord/Be here and and everywhere adored;

These creatures bless and grant that we/May feast in Paradise with thee.

John Wesley is an inspiration, (and I am not a Methodist). He rode horseback back and forth throughout England preaching and establishing Methodism. He traveled many, many hundreds of miles to do this... and even came to America to preach as well. He, along with some of his other followers, brought Methodism to America. If we act on our convictions, we *will* move out of despondency. Reading biographies of active and committed people can be inspiring and motivating and can help us to get moving again.

An achievement today is _____

_____

_____

OCTOBER 28

...Do you not see all these things?...

– Matthew 24: 2

In Louisiana, there is much preparation for All Saints' Day. The tombs are whitewashed, and fresh flowers placed upon them. The cemeteries are lavish with color and brilliant sparkling white in the days before All Saints'. (November 1). Families gather around the tombstones of their dead and work together, scrubbing, whitewashing, and putting fresh flowers on the gravesites. The state has a multitude of centuries old tombs, and most are well maintained and looked after. Then, on All Saints' Day, the community turns out for the blessing of the tombs. It's a peaceful, beautiful event to witness if there's such a tradition in your locality as well.

An achievement today is_____

_____

_____

_____

_____

_____

_____

_____

OCTOBER 29

...a disciple of the kingdom of heaven is like a head of a household, who brings out of his treasure things new and old.
– Matthew 13: 52

If you've reviewed the Elijah story recently, then you will recall the details of what transpired between Elijah and the widow. There had been a long drought and subsequent famine. She had almost nothing for her and her son, but Elijah asked her to make him a little cake from her pittance of grain. She did so, and then he told her to ask neighbors for empty vessels so she could fill them with the little bit of oil she had remaining. She was able to fill all the empty vessels with that little bit of oil and this kept her going for the rest of those hard times. A period of depression may seem like a long drought, and then one day we notice it's over, and happiness can flow again just like the never ending oil of the Elijah story.

An achievement today is_____

_____

_____

_____

_____

OCTOBER 30

...It is more blessed to give than to receive.

– Acts 20: 35

Did you know that the only place this quote of Jesus is written is not in the Gospels, but in Acts? We have heard this quote so many times, that it would be easy to think it was in the Gospels. However, the teaching about giving is something we have all been told many times...that giving is better than receiving. Yet often we are reluctant to let go of something we want to hang onto, despite the conviction that God wants us to give it! I've found that if I have such a conviction and don't give something when I feel I'm supposed to, that I lose it or it is ruined somehow. So, I've learned if I feel I'm being directed to give something, that I'd better give it, because if I don't, I'm going to lose it anyway!

Something I felt I was supposed to give_____

_____

_____

_____

_____

_____

_____

_____

OCTOBER 31

I do not speak to all of you. I know the ones I have chosen; but it is that the Scripture may be fulfilled, 'He who eats my bread has lifted up his heel against Me.'

–John 13: 18

Have you ever been betrayed? By someone close to you, or someone you trusted? If we have been betrayed, we need to be on guard that we don't become bitter because of the actions of this one person. Bitterness does nothing for us, doesn't change the past, and yet it does change the future because it doesn't let in the light. Rather, it keeps us in the shadows. One of my friends was shocked to discover that her attorney son had stolen substantially from her trust fund. In addition to that story, another woman I know was deceived out of her entire inheritance by *her* attorney son. Recognize that there will always be untrustworthy and deceitful persons. (Jesus called them vipers and wolves.) We do our best to avoid them; but we need to stay open to the ethical people...and there are millions of those good people out there.

An achievement today is_____

_____

_____

NOVEMBER I

...Blessed are those who did not see, and yet believed.
– John 20: 29

Nothing against pedicures, but I know some women who pay more attention to the color of the polish on their toes than they do their spiritual life. A life spent at the beauty salon can take hundreds of hours and hundreds of dollars for facials, hair treatments, manicures, and pedicures, and that's okay for someone who wants to spend all that time and money. But, is an equal amount of energy or more spent on studying and learning and meditating? Another way of looking at this is: Is as much energy spent on the internal self as on the external self? Time spent on the internal will produce beauty of a more lasting nature, and this will be highly visible on the external self.

An achievement today is_____

_____

_____

_____

_____

_____

_____

_____

NOVEMBER 2

*...When you were younger you used to gird yourself and
walk wherever you wished...*

– John 21: 18

I was considered a Tomboy when I was a child. I loved
to skip stones across the creek, collect minnows and
fireflies in Mason jars, and go on various adventures,
especially camping along the Jersey Shore. If you're
looking for something different to do, consider finding yourself a creek or a river, and then look for small
flat stones to skip along the surface. The more times
you can get a stone to skip across the water, the better.
This is an occupation that can bring relaxation and
peace for hours...and it's really fun to do. Your inner
child will no doubt love it too. And remember, what
your inner child loves to do will brighten your eyes and
invigorate you immediately! (and also strengthen your
immune system and increase your creativity.)

A favorite activity when I was a child was_____

_____

_____

_____

_____

_____

NOVEMBER 3

...and He will send forth His angels...
– Matthew 24: 31

Driving north on a divided four lane highway, my tire went off the side of the road and because of the soft shoulder was hurled onto the steep incline of the median. My brakes wouldn't work although I was frantically pumping them. My little girl was napping with her head on my lap as we hurtled down the incline toward the opposite side of the Interstate where cars and big rigs were roaring along at high speeds. Then, miraculously the car suddenly stopped *on the incline.* Truckers had stopped alongside the highway because they were so sure I was headed toward a major collision on the other side. "We thought you were done for," exclaimed the driver of a big rig. "Somebody's looking out for you!" The truckers helped me get back onto the Interstate and into traffic flow once more. Since then I've never doubted that we have guardian angels!

A close call that I've had is_____

_____

_____

_____

_____

NOVEMBER 4

So take care then how you listen...
 – Luke 8: 18

Humming is good for us. In the book, *Change Your Brain, Change Your Life,* Daniel Amen discusses this. Whistling also is beneficial and improves our mood. Remember Jimminy Cricket singing *Whistle While You Work?* Just as vibrations carried by music can realign and balance our cells, so whistling and humming vibrations can benefit body and mind as well. And increase needed energy and lift our mood. That cliché of whistling past the graveyard can be understood on many different levels. If we're anxious about something, whistling or humming can relax us. My daughter, a professional singer and voice coach, strongly believes whistling and humming are great for improving mood and physical well being.

A tune I like to hum or whistle is_____
_____
_____
_____
_____
_____
_____

NOVEMBER 5

...Tend my lambs.

–John 21: 15

Don't believe that cynical saying: "No good deed goes unpunished". Even if we are experiencing a low mood, we can still bring encouragement to another who is suffering and needs some attention. Remember Jesus directs us to visit the sick and those in prison. I have unsung friends who have spent decades quietly visiting inmates and bringing them hope. A retired doctor friend is one of a group of retired doctors that goes to facilities in their Florida community to treat elders. Or maybe you have a neighbor who could use a bit of help or a kind act. One thing is for sure...when we help others, we are invariably going to elevate our mood.

Someone who could use my help today is_____

_____

_____

_____

_____

_____

_____

_____

NOVEMBER 6

...the seed is the word of God.

– Luke 8: 11

In her book, *Growing Myself,* Judith Handelsman writes about working with plants as a means to getting beyond a time of upheaval and pain. If you have a yard and can garden, that's terrific. If you don't, and are only able to grow plants in an apartment, she has ideas for that as well in her book, *How to Grow Plants from Recycled Kitchen Scraps.* Always keeping an eye out for interesting glass bottles, my windowsills are crowded with these as I attempt to root all sorts of plants in them. I make it a point to visit all my plants daily, whether outdoors or indoors, in order to check on them.

They may need water, or some dead leaves or blossoms pinched off. As we care for plants, pets, or people, we are getting out of ourselves and thereby improving our mood. Some people claim, "I kill plants. Everything I try to grow dies on me." When I hear this, I always reply, "Start with the easy plants." There's a long list of them, and your local garden center will help you select these.

Plants I would like to grow are_____

_____

_____

NOVEMBER 7

...Sit at My right hand...
– Matthew 22: 44

Are you right brained or left brained? We're all a combination, but some of us are more strongly one way or the other. If you're strongly right brained, you may have felt out of the loop in many situations because our culture caters mostly to the predominantly left-brained individual. A tidy workspace with everything put away neatly is often an indication that a left brain works there. A workplace with piles and stacks of paper or other working materials on it suggests that a right brain works there. A book that describes the tyranny of the left brain work world is: *A Perfect Mess: The Hidden Benefits of Disorder* by Abrahamson and Freedman. If you're right brained, this book will encourage you about how messiness can aid and promote success in your thinking and your endeavors. If you're left brained, this book will help you to loosen up a bit and unleash your creativity. Whether you work in a messy environment or a neat one, making progress toward our goals will always improve our moods.

Some progress I made today toward a goal is_____

NOVEMBER 8

...All things are possible for You...
– Mark 14: 36

Neuro-linguistic Programming, or NLP, teaches Anchoring. An example of anchoring is this: You feel drowsy, so you press a certain spot on your body... maybe on your hand, maybe on your arm or leg, to anchor the drowsy feeling. Then, next time you want to feel that way, you press that very same spot...and amazingly, you will start to feel drowsy! Same technique can be used if you want to feel wide awake. So, if you have a spot on one arm for drowsy, and the other for wide awake, you have a built in automatic system for either feeling. The more you practice using your anchoring spots, the faster the technique will work for you. There's much, much more to NLP than anchoring, but for the purpose of improving our moods, anchoring can be used next time you feel really good. Press a certain spot on hand, arm, or leg to anchor that good feeling. And it really works!

An achievement today is_____
_____
_____
_____

NOVEMBER 9

... John came to you in the way of righteousness, and you did not believe him; but the tax collectors and prostitutes did believe him...

– Matthew 21: 32

If you believe, as millions do, that you are supposed to be doing something meaningful here on earth, then what would that be? If you haven't a clue, this may be a good time to think about it. Or maybe not think about it, and just let the answer float up to the surface from deep within, kind of like that toy, Magic 8 Ball. If you sit quietly and blank your mind, you may get an answer to the question, "What am I supposed to be doing with my life?" Maybe you are already doing it, maybe not. But it's a beneficial exercise if you're at a crossroads and need some answers. With all the distractions of modern day life, often our inner self has a hard time getting through to us. A recent list of statistics reports that the average man spends eleven years of his life watching television. Talk about distractions!

Meaningful work to me is_____
_____
_____
_____

NOVEMBER 10

...and the man was speechless.

– Matthew 22: 12

We always have the choice of switching our inner dial to a peaceful frequency, or else remaining in a state of discomfort, static, and free-floating anxiety. Fine tuning our inner "radio dial" will invariably get us to a better place. Some days this is easier to do than others, of course, but no matter what is occurring in our life, we *can* turn that inner dial. And the more we practice fine-tuning our inner frequency, the easier it will be to find a peaceful "station." The biggest problem with shedding addictions for those who struggle with this, is that the addict doesn't know how to adjust his/her inner dial. And the addict typically is unwilling to feel discomfort, so will rush to do most anything to obtain the D.O.C. or drug of choice, rather than learn how to feel good inside naturally. Learning to operate our inner radio dial is crucial if we want to improve our mood.

An achievement today is_____

_____

_____

_____

_____

NOVEMBER 12

I will give you the keys of the kingdom of heaven…
– Matthew 16: 19

Weather conditions have a lot to do with our mood, especially for those who are sensitive to this. Drizzly overcast days can help maintain a relaxed mood. Low pressure days can cause headaches and tension. People sensitive to phases of the moon may notice increased tension during periods of full moon. Heavy humidity may sap your energy so that you feel like you're slogging through the day. You may feel heightened good mood during bright sunny days…especially if you get outside and enjoy the fresh air and light. Become aware of how you react to different weather conditions. An excellent book on the subject is: *Your Health, Your Moods, and the Weather* by W.S. Kals.

I am mood sensitive to weather that is_____

_____

_____

_____

_____

_____

_____

NOVEMBER 13

And when you are praying, do not use meaningless repetition as the Gentiles do, for they suppose that they will be heard for their many words.

– Matthew 6: 7

Toning is a technique used by singers to warm up. Try it. It's good for you, and for your daily tune-up. Toning is helpful for our inner space. Practice saying the vowels out loud, but drag out the sounds of each one for at least five seconds. Feel the vibration of each pronounced vowel deep within your abdomen. Say the A as in Aaaaaaaaah, then Eeeeeeeeee, Iiiiiiiiiiii, Ooooooo, Uuuuuuuuuuu. This inner vibration is healing and balancing and grounding. Toning will help to stabilize shifting up and down moods. Toning also increases our sense of well being and helps to decrease worry and anxiety. Practice toning during the day as often as needed. If you're surrounded by people and can't do it out loud, do it internally. This will also have an effect. You won't feel the healing vibration, but it is calming nevertheless.

An achievement today is_____

_____

_____

_____

NOVEMBER 14

Blessed are the peacemakers, for they shall be called sons of God.

– Matthew 5: 9

Once we are experiencing a good inner feeling, and we are enjoying the peace and serenity of it, we need to learn how to maintain it. We need to learn how to stay with the feeling of serenity, rather than chase off after another distraction. Maybe we are feeling really good, then along comes another set of negative thoughts that trip us up and seduce us back into inner static and circular worry thoughts. However, we *can* learn how to bypass these distractions and remain with that good inner feeling. We *always* have a choice when it comes to our inner status. But we have to learn how we stop ourselves from experiencing peace and serenity. How we self-sabotage our inner emotional landscape. *I always have a choice. I always have a choice.* This is a mantra that we can all practice whenever we find ourselves disturbed by unwelcome thoughts.

An achievement today is_____

_____

_____

_____

NOVEMBER 15

...Call the laborers and pay them their wages...
– Matthew 20: 8

Doing something with our hands can be calming. Some people like to do needle-work or quilting. Some like to work on small engines. Some engage in wood-working.

Some make models such as airplanes. There are a multitude of ways to engage in handwork. Using our hands has an effect on our brain and consequently our moods. Just recently, I learned how to make tortillas by hand (had to throw that in as a possibility because it's such fun to do). Of course practicing any instrument involves hand/mind coordination. The importance of this is explained in *Change Your Brain, Change Your Life* by Daniel Amen, M.D., a truly fascinating book, which I highly recommend.

Something I like to do with my hands is_____

_____

_____

_____

_____

_____

_____

NOVEMBER 16

For the gate is small and the way is narrow that leads to life,
and there are few who find it.

– Matthew 7: 14

There are so many different kinds of depression: Major, Situational, Hormonal, Reactive, Seasonal, Dysthymic, Unipolar. Diet, Sunshine, and Exercise help to decrease all types of depression. And that's common knowledge and common sense. I would add making some progress on our goals to that list. If every day we are doing something toward our long term and short term goals, then we will improve our moods. If we take a moment to enjoy the good feeling of closure when we do complete a task, we will improve our mood. If we learn to stay with those times when we enjoy the humming warm feeling of being *in tune*, we will be able to maintain a good mood. We *can* learn to do this. And learning to do this is critical to our sense of well being.

An achievement today is_____

_____

_____

_____

_____

_____

NOVEMBER 17

Blessed are the gentle, for they shall inherit the earth.

– Matthew 5: 5

Wisdom literature for centuries has advised us to not identify with our ego. Yet, this is easier said than done when still feeling hurt or wounded from someone's rejection or mean, maybe even cruel remark. However, it can help to know that whenever we feel hurt, the ego *is always involved.* We need the ego because that is how we present ourselves to the world. However, it is important to remember that we don't have to identify with our persona. We can look upon it as a mask or a costume that we wear in the world. What we really are, is a bright and shining soul. This body is kind of like wearing a suit, and it's best not to get too worked up about it. Those people who spend much time per day looking in the mirror, consumed by how they look, worrying about it so much they resort to going under the knife for plastic surgery need to lighten up. Look at your body as a necessary space suit for moving through life, and focus instead on your shining soul, because that's what *really* shows through.

An achievement today is_____

_____

_____

NOVEMBER 18

*...worry of the world and the deceitfulness of wealth choke
the word, and it becomes unfruitful.*

– Matthew 13: 22

The wise saying that good things come out of bad times
has certainly proved true in my life. As an experiment, take
a hard look at the rough times you have gone through in
your life in the past, and see what has come out of the turmoil. You may find some good things came out of those
learning experiences. Maybe you were forced to take a
new direction, follow a new path. Maybe you were able to
let go of some things or people that you realize now were
not good for you. Maybe you learned some valuable lessons that have helped you avoid further adverse circumstances. Maybe those unfortunate times helped you to
rely on and go deeper into your faith. Other familiar sayings are: *After the rain clouds comes the sunshine,* and *Everything happens for a reason.* These old sayings have become
clichés, however, they have endured because they have
proven true so many times to so many people.

Something good that came out of a rough situation for
me is_____
_____
_____

NOVEMBER 19

... I feel compassion for the people...
– Matthew 15: 32

In order to realize the desires of our heart, we first have to *know* the desires of our heart.

What is it you most want to have happen? If you aren't sure, then ponder that for a few minutes. What we want in life may not come about in the same way that we think. We may be surprised by the way life works our desires out for us. And we may be surprised by the length of time it takes. It may happen faster than we think, or take much longer than we expected. The most fulfilling way to conduct our life is not to be focused on outcomes, but rather on the process of getting there. If we can learn to enjoy the work as we move toward our goals, we will not be so impatient for the outcome to occur. Human nature wants whatever it is we desire NOW. But that's a sure road to frustration and the restless feelings of impatience. And when feeling impatient, we are missing the beauties all around us that occur every day.

Something I enjoyed doing today_____

_____

_____

NOVEMBER 20

…Many will come from east and west…
– Matthew 8: 11

Millions of people enjoy watching and playing games that use a ball. Soccer, football, baseball, softball, basketball, golf, pool, ice hockey, field hockey, polo, volleyball, bowling, La Crosse, tennis, ping-pong, racketball. It's a long list. If there's a ball game going on in your area, maybe you could participate or attend. Whether the game's at a school, in a park, or on the beach, it can't help but improve your mood to be joining in with the excitement and fun of a game. And the high energy of the players and the spectators is contagious. Ball games invariably elevate a down mood. Even if it's not your thing, you might consider giving it a try. Your inner child will thank you for it.

Something fun that I did today is_____

_____

_____

_____

_____

_____

_____

_____

NOVEMBER 21

...finds it unoccupied, swept, and put in order.
– Matthew 12: 44

A Native-American technique for clearing the house of sad or discordant "vibes," is to "smoke" the house. Heat some dried sage in a skillet so that it smokes. Then carry the still smoking skillet into each room of the house, letting the good smelling smoke drift throughout the living space. This leaves a refreshing aroma of sage that is pleasant and clears the air. You can buy sage wrapped in a small bundle for this purpose in specialty stores, or you can just sprinkle sage from a spice can into the skillet. I use a black cast iron pan for this, and have used both the sage bundle, fresh sage from the garden, and dry sage from a spice bottle. This technique helps to dissipate the residue of a period of despondency, and helps us move on into a period of improved mood and higher energy. (My daughter calls this a bit of *sage* advice.)

An achievement today is_____
_____
_____
_____
_____

NOVEMBER 22

...does he not leave the ninety-nine on the mountains and go and search for the one that is straying?

– Matthew 18: 12

If you believe that coincidences demonstrate God's sense of humor, then you probably cherish them as I do. Once while on a car trip of six hundred miles, my beloved 1965 Mustang developed engine trouble. I pulled off by the side of the road near to a construction site. The construction workers were building an apartment house. I walked over to the nearest carpenter and explained to him that I was having car trouble and asked if he knew a good mechanic in the area. It turned out this man was an old friend of one of my close friends who lives in Arizona! He immediately arranged for me to meet with a mechanic who had me up and running by the next day. What are the odds of me finding a friend of a friend out of the hundreds of thousands of residents of the city of Tallahassee, six hundred miles from home? Not only do I believe that God has a sense of humor, but also that these coincidences assure us that we are indeed being looked after.

A coincidence that has happened to me is_____

NOVEMBER 22

and they did not understand until the flood came and took them all away...

– Matthew 24: 39

In the book, *Your Health, Your Moods, and the Weather,* W.S. Kals writes in detail about the effects of a combination of high humidity and low barometric pressure. This causes millions of people to hurt owing to arthritis, rheumatism and other physical conditions. Aches and pains, stiffness and headaches do not help us maintain a good mood. However, it's helpful to be aware of the weather connection to the discomfort so we can better deal with it. For example, if you are aware that you are weather sensitive, and that certain conditions are going to affect your mood, then it's easier to shrug the discomfort off and carry on in spite of it, as we tell ourselves: *It's just the weather!* We have no control over the weather; we *do* have control over our moods.

An achievement today is_____
_____
_____
_____
_____
_____

NOVEMBER 23

...To you has been given the mystery of the kingdom of God...

– Mark 4: 11

Thanksgiving is a time of celebration and a time for gratitude. If we have been regularly feeling grateful for the blessings of each day, then on Thanksgiving we are doing no more than we usually do regarding gratitude. Some books recommend writing down what we are grateful for each day. Making these lists creates an *attitude of gratitude* as 12-Step groups put it. An attitude of gratitude will do so much more for our sense of well being than a complaining or blaming attitude. All this gets us is more to complain about and more to blame about...a recipe for a sour mood if ever there was one. Listing what we are grateful for will improve our mood and bring more goodness into our life.

Something I am especially grateful for today is_____

_____

_____

_____

_____

_____

_____

NOVEMBER 24

...Who touched my garments?

– Mark 5: 30

Touch that feels good enhances brain activity. Wearing fabrics that feel good can be helpful to improve mood. Soft cottons, wools, and flannels will do more for us than scratchy fabrics or wearing something that makes us itch. Some of us are allergic to detergents and fabric softeners, and wearing clothes, sleeping on sheets, or using towels that carry a residue of these chemicals can have an adverse affect. It helps to run a wash with sheets and clothes without using detergent at all. There is so much left over detergent and fabric softeners from previous washings that running washes with sheets, towels and clothes, but no detergent, can clear away much of this residue buildup. If you are sensitive to chemicals, try using washing soda instead of detergent, and forget the fabric softeners altogether. You may find this simple change will improve your sleep, your skin, and your moods. (I speak from personal experience, as I'm very sensitive to household chemicals. Many others are too, but aren't aware of it.)

An achievement today is_____

NOVEMBER 25

...You give them something to eat!...
– Mark 6: 37

If you've already included L-trytophan in your diet, then you've most likely discovered how this amino acid is calming. Meat, especially turkey, eggs, potatoes, and milk all contain L-tryptophan. Serotonin is often at low levels in depressed people, and L-tryptophan helps to enhance serotonin production. There's a good reason why a traditional Thanksgiving dinner with roast turkey and mashed potatoes ends with the guests asleep on the couch afterwards. Exercise also enhances serotonin production. If you've been accelerating your exercise program, you have no doubt noticed improved mood and enhanced sense of well being.

An achievement today is_____

_____

_____

_____

_____

_____

_____

_____

NOVEMBER 26

Blessed are you who hunger now, for you shall be satisfied...
— Luke 6: 21

Negative thoughts, depressed mood, and low energy can also be aggravated by low norepinephrine and dopamine levels. Protein snacks and avoiding sugar helps with this.

And, of course, exercise will help to get our inner chemistry flowing again. Different types of exercise help with different areas. We need cardiovascular exercise to keep our heart muscle strong and pumping blood, and oxygen circulating, and our lungs working fully, instead of that shallow breathing so frequent with depressed mood.

We can use light weights to tone our muscles. I'm partial to a small weight ball for upper body work, but go easy at first; a little bit of weight workout goes a long way in the beginning.

Some exercise I did today is_____

_____

_____

_____

_____

_____

NOVEMBER 27

...will not God bring about justice for His elect who cry to Him day and night...

– Luke 18: 7

People who are depressed are not much fun to be around; in fact, studies have shown that most people tend to avoid depressed individuals. So if you are aware that you have been isolating and spiraling further down into the dumps, you may also get the feeling that your friends have begun to leave you alone. I'm not suggesting putting on a false face, but certainly working our support system, exercising, and expanding our activities outside of the house and into the community are going to help us get through any down and out period faster. Often a depressed person thinks mistakenly that they are helpless against this wave of despondency. This is one of the lies of the distorted thinking of depression. Recovery from depression is in our hands. We have to put forth the effort to do the things we know will make us feel better. No matter how low we feel, we *must* make the effort and get off the couch, and out of the shadows of the house. It's entirely up to us to do this. No one can do it for us.

An effort I made today is_____

_____

NOVEMBER 28

for I will give you utterance and wisdom which none of your opponents will be able to resist or refute.

– Luke 21: 15

You know the old saying, "Be careful how you treat people on the way up, cause you'll meet them again on the way down." Well, if we've been down, then we're going to be going up...that's for sure. So now that you're on the way up, be sure to be extra nice to everyone you meet from here on! Don't forget, you're making ripples wherever you go. If you're pleasant to everyone you meet, even if they are not, you will engage the ripple effect. Maybe that not so pleasant person had a lousy morning, and your friendliness helped them to feel better. Now they're going to pass on their improved mood to the next person they meet. It's all a chain reaction, and you know what they say....we're all connected by only nine degrees of separation. So your behavior in even the smallest interaction today has far reaching, rippling effects.

An achievement today is_____

_____

_____

_____

NOVEMBER 29

Blessed are the pure in heart, for they shall see God.

– Matthew 5: 8

No matter what the distortion of a down mood is telling you…there are millions of loving, honest, conscientious people in the world. An old friend of mine goes to Mexico often to buy pottery. He's an expert on the subject and travels all over the country to find the pieces he wants. Once in a small mountain village, he paid for his lunch and was headed out of town. A man came running after him calling to him to stop. Bill did, and went back to where the man was. He had made a mistake and substantially overpaid him, and the villager wanted to give him his change before he left town!

An especially kind act that someone did for me was_____

_____

_____

_____

_____

_____

_____

_____

_____

NOVEMBER 30

For nothing is hidden, except to be revealed...
– Mark 4: 22

If you've been paying attention to your dreams and keeping a dream diary, perhaps you've noticed a change in your dream life. The more attention we give to our dreams, the more we are going to remember them and understand them. Bear in mind, that some of the most important inventions of mankind have come through the dreams of the inventors. A dream led to Crick and Watson's understanding of DNA. A dream led to the invention of the sewing machine. Coleridge dreamed the famous poem, "Kubla Khan" in its entirety, but unfortunately was only able to remember part of it because a stranger knocking on his door interrupted him before he could write it all down. Keep paying attention to your dreams, and honor them by writing down what you can remember. And ask for dream guidance in matters that concern you before you go to sleep at night. You will be glad you took the time to do these things.

A revealing dream I've had is_____

_____

_____

DECEMBER I

…You were faithful with a few things, I will put you in charge of many things…

– Matthew 25: 21

A longtime friend of mine whose word I trust, reports that one day alone at home, he clearly heard a voice ordering him to GO! He knew exactly what the voice meant. Get to the hospital immediately. He got in his truck and drove to the Emergency Room, parked, and as he walked inside the doors, he passed out and fell down. The staff rushed him into treatment and saved his life. The doctor told him he had a heart attack, and would have died had he not immediately heeded the firm order to GO. My friend, believing he had received divine guidance, had immediately obeyed when he heard the voice. This is one more example of the importance of staying alert to our guidance. But, if we don't practice quieting our run-on thoughts, we may not hear it. *There are none so deaf as those who won't hear!*

A time that I received critical guidance was _____

_____

_____

_____

_____

DECEMBER 2

...this generation will not pass away until all these things take place.

– Matthew 24: 34

We are a mixture of genes from our parents, grandparents, and even further back. The particular mix that is us is unique, however. In addition to genetic predispositions, we may find, as many people do, that a lot of what we choose to do is in response to our parents' or grandparents' behaviors. For example, someone whose mother was a fastidious housekeeper may go in the opposite direction...as a response to all that over-the-top cleaning. Someone whose parent was a workaholic may respond by doing as little work as possible. Someone whose parent was a compulsive gambler may never even play a game of cards or enter a casino. Then, of course, there are those who respond by emulating their forebears in all sorts of ways. That old saying, *The acorn falls close to the tree,* speaks to that. However you respond to your heritage, it's a good thing to become aware of how you are doing that, and in what ways.

A response to my parents has been_____

_____

_____

DECEMBER 3

...Do you not see all these things?...
– Matthew 24: 2

Doing routine things in a different way is good brain exercise. It helps to keep the intricate connections of the brain flowing. Try doing something with your other hand that you usually do with your favored hand. Try taking a different route than you usually do as you drive somewhere. Experiment with your routine. Shake it up a bit, and notice how this makes you feel. Changing our customary way of doing things is not only good brain exercise, we may also discover new preferences. Changing our routine, and the same old, same old, may also lead to fresh insights. What's more, as we nurture new pathways in the brain, we may even come up with an invention or two. Countless inventions have come about because the inventor accidentally stumbled upon a *new* way of looking at things.

Something I did differently today is_____

_____

_____

_____

_____

_____

DECEMBER 4

...It is written, 'You shall worship the Lord your God, and serve Him only.'

– Luke 4: 8

A concept I like very much from Judeo-Christian tradition is that every action we take brings us further toward God, or further away from God. I believe we usually know the answer to this as we proceed through our day. A peaceful feeling of contentment is a good indication that what we're doing at the moment is leading us toward God. A nagging, draining feeling of conscience or unrest as we're doing something is probably a good indication that we're moving in the opposite direction, and away from God. Our learning to discern between the two directions is a useful practice. The more we pay attention to this, the more we will catch ourselves going down a path that will not benefit us. Sometimes we may be aware of doing something that moves us away from God and being tempted, may choose to do it anyway. But the more we choose to move toward God, the more we will enjoy peace, rather than discord and turmoil.

An achievement today is_____

_____

_____

DECEMBER 5

...repent, and believe in the gospel.

– Mark 1: 15

On the subject of temptation, knowing our limitations can be useful. For example, I recognize that I am weak when it comes to certain foods, so I never have them in the house. If I want to be able to fit into my favorite jeans, I can't have peanut butter, ice cream, chips, or other such delectables in the house, because I'll tear right through them. If we trigger any weakness or addiction, we are giving new energy to a part of our personality that has no brakes. And if we do at times trigger an addictive part of our personality, we are going to suffer for it by way of a lowdown mood later. Keeping tempting things out of the house entirely, staying away from risky situations, and being mindful of our weaknesses, can go a long way toward maintaining a stable mood.

A temptation I have learned to avoid is_____

_____

_____

_____

_____

_____

DECEMBER 6

…What is written in the Law? How does it read to you?
— Luke 10: 26

Memorizing license plates is a brain exercise I enjoy. I get better and better at it the more I practice doing it. There are times when we may need to have memorized a license plate, for example as a witness to a hit and run, or as part of a Neighborhood Watch Program. I find as I practice over time, that I have found ways of doing this successfully, such as repeating it over and over to myself until I've been able to write it down. Also remembering the number configuration visually, like a snapshot, is helpful until it's written down. It pays to practice attentiveness, and it's good brain calisthenics. (I used to tell myself I couldn't memorize a group of numbers quickly, until I began practicing it. Never say can't!)
Brain exercise helps us move on out of a stalled period quicker!

An achievement today is_____
_____
_____
_____
_____

DECEMBER 7

…Do not fear; from now on you will be catching men.

– Luke 5: 10

Do you find yourself living on the edge, waiting for the shoe to drop?

Do you have a feeling of dread that something bad is going to happen?

Are you good at catastrophic thinking? Try retraining your mind to live with the expectation that something great is going to happen. That you are going to be surprised by something wonderful very soon. Start looking for the beauty all around you, instead of what offends you. *We get more of what we put our attention on.* By this I mean that if we think the world is a dangerous place, and people are untrustworthy, we will find more and more examples that prove our point. If, on the other hand, we keep looking around for beauty and goodness, we will find it shimmering everywhere.

Something beautiful I saw today is_____

_____

_____

_____

_____

_____

DECEMBER 8

...This man began to build and was not able to finish.

— Luke 14: 30

Studies have shown that optimists succeed more in life than pessimists. This is irrespective of IQ or school grades. If going through a low period, we may have a rather dismal outlook on our future because the depressed feelings distort our vision. If becoming aware that you are looking at the dark side, and minimizing your prospects, turn that thinking around by reminding yourself that your thinking is temporarily on the bleak side, but there is light ahead. Going through a rough patch is *temporary!* There will be bright colors, joy, wonders, and laughter shortly. Maybe even as soon as today!

A bright spot in my day is_____

_____

_____

_____

_____

_____

_____

_____

DECEMBER 9

Those on the rocky soil are those who, when they hear, receive the word with joy; and these have no firm root; they believe for a while, and in time of temptation fall away.

– Luke 8: 13

Two neighbors of mine were working out in their yard. The one man looked downcast, and I asked him how he was doing. The other man gently said, "He wants to be depressed today." Even though we may not think it's true, we *do* have a choice about feeling depressed or not on any given day. And we *can* learn to feel happy rather than indulging in low spirits. A question to ask is: how do I know when I'm happy? What would be the indicators or clues? Contemplate this, and then emulate some of those symptoms of happiness. It's often been said that when we smile, our mood actually changes for the better, even if we were feeling low. Whenever I catch myself drooping and trudging through the day, I make myself put some PEP in my STEP. This always raises my spirits, no matter how tired I may feel. This may sound a bit simplistic, but it truly works.

A clue that I am feeling happy is_____
_____
_____

DECEMBER 10

…You have answered correctly; do this and you will live.

– Luke 10: 28

There's a line from the song, *I Can't Drive Fifty-Five,"* that goes like this:
"I've got one foot on the brake and one foot on the gas." This sounds to me like the stalled condition we may be in at times. We need to take our foot off the brake, and quit stopping ourself from moving forward. Those stalled times we need to give it some gas! Put the pedal to the metal! I know this is easier to say than to do if we're in downtime or low energy mode. However, only *we* can take our foot off the brake and start working on some of the things we want to accomplish. Even if it's just a small accomplishment, we will feel good about at last getting it done, and this good feeling will lead us into even more positive actions tomorrow.

An achievement today is_____

_____

_____

_____

_____

_____

DECEMBER 11

...I must preach the kingdom of God to the other cities also, for I was sent for this purpose.

– Luke 4: 43

During the season of Advent, some people feel overwhelmed by the demands of the Christmas season. One woman I know, a perfectionist, drives herself to distraction because she insists on doing so much for her family and friends that she exhausts herself. If the holidays are a trying time for you, cut back and recognize your limitations. Do what you decide to do for the season by increments. A little bit here, and a little bit there, and what you want to do gets done. It's a season for giving, so give yourself a break.

An achievement today is_____

_____

_____

_____

_____

_____

_____

_____

_____

_____

DECEMBER 12

...Do not hinder him, for he who is not against you is for you.

– Luke 9: 50

When I was a teenager, a very influential person in my life, Tom Chamales, a writer, stressed this to me. "No matter how many times you get knocked down in life, you have to keep getting back up." All these years later, I still have this vivid memory of Tom gravely telling me this. He died tragically just a few years later, but I've never forgotten this important lesson. And it has helped me get back up and get through any calamities in my life. Is there some vital lesson you were taught by someone when you were growing up that has stuck with you through the years and helped you to "get back up"?

Something that has helped me is_____
_____
_____
_____
_____
_____
_____
_____

DECEMBER 13

...Are you the teacher of Israel and do not understand these things?

– John 3: 10

Hannukah is a Festival of Lights. If there is a Hannukuh event planned in your area, this is an activity that is fun to attend and very lovely. Ever mindful that Jesus was Jewish, I pay attention to Jewish holidays. If you have Jewish friends, you might send them a Hannukah card, and even light candles during the eight days. As part of our Judeo-Christian tradition, this is a beautiful and a giving holiday... on many levels.

An achievement today is_____

_____
_____
_____
_____
_____
_____
_____
_____
_____

DECEMBER 14

Those whom I love......

– Revelation 3: 19

In the story of Samson and Delilah, Samson was victim to Delilah's treachery and revealed the secret of his strength to her. Through her deceit and cunning, she learned that she could cut his hair and thus weaken him. What she didn't count on was that his hair would grow back while in captivity, and so would his superhuman strength. What are your strengths? Have you been utilizing your strengths lately? If you've been going through a rough time, you may have forgotten where your strengths lie. While it's good to be aware of our limitations, we need to use our resources as well. Make a list of all your strengths. You may be surprised at just how long a list you come up with.

One of my strengths that I've not used lately is_____

_____

_____

_____

_____

_____

_____

_____

DECEMBER 15

For if you believed Moses, you would believe Me, for he wrote about Me. But if you do not believe his writings, how will you believe My words?

– John 5: 46, 47

As you assess your strengths, you may want to go over the list with a trusted friend. Your friend might want to add a strength or two that they have seen in you, but you have not. Your friend might want to make a list of his/her own strengths and show it to you for feedback. This exercise might prove fruitful as you move forward. Part of working our support system includes using our strengths as well. And being aware of our strengths is the first step toward doing this. Sometimes a person may discover a strength they didn't know they had during an emergency. They may find they act while others stand frozen in shock or fear. During a period of depression, a person may be so self-critical, they overlook their strengths. This is still another example of the distorted thinking that is a by-product of depression.

One of my strengths is _____

_____

_____

_____

DECEMBER 16

...for everyone who exalts himself will be humbled...
– Luke 18: 14

Franz Schubert, the famous composer, was said to struggle with depression. Yet he composed so much music that it would be difficult for a person to even hear it all. And he died so very young, at thirty-one, leaving his voluminous works behind for us. Here's another example of an individual who transformed uncomfortable feelings into energy for abundant creativity. If you listen to your favorite music for long enough periods of time, your mind will be filled with music long after you turn it off, owing to auditory memory.

Music is so much more beneficial and enjoyable than listening on and on to gloomy, anxious thoughts. Next time you notice you're giving in to a negative mindset, put on some music and override that useless, dismal train of thought.

An achievement today is_____
_____
_____
_____
_____
_____

DECEMBER 17

As Moses lifted up the serpent in the wilderness, even so must the Son of Man be lifted up.

—John 3: 14

Do you put yourself down? Some people often do this when interacting with others. Comments such as, "Oh, I hate my hair!" or "I'm so stupid, forgetful, clumsy," etc. Being humble is one thing; self-deprecating is another. I suspect that those who do this in public also do it to themselves privately. If you catch yourself doing this, counter it with statements of self-appreciation. Self conscious statements such as, "I can't dance," can become, "I'm getting better at it all the time." Knowing our limitations is one thing; being willing to expand our capabilities is another.

Something I want to get better at is_____

_____

_____

_____

_____

_____

_____

_____

DECEMBER 18

...A prophet is not without honor except in his hometown and among his own relatives and in his own household.

– Mark 6: 4

Some people make mean-spirited comments under the guise of being concerned. For example, saying to someone in the workplace, "You look tired," or "Have you been sick?" If you know someone who often does this sort of thing, stay clear of them if you can. This sort of behavior does not help to improve anyone's mood, and can be draining to someone who is trying their best to do their job. Persons who subtly work against others are dealing with their own miseries, or they wouldn't make such comments. Remember, when we're feeling great inside, we feel kindness towards all, and we project that as well. And people can feel that good will just by being near us. We broadcast it just as surely as if we're a working radio station.

An achievement today is_____

_____

_____

_____

_____

_____

DECEMBER 19

...Not all men can accept this statement, but only those to whom it has been given.

– Matthew 19: 11

If you've been exercising several times a week, that's terrific. However, do not be a "weekend warrior," and do too much all at once. If we overdo and get stiff, aching muscles because of it, we may not get back out there again for days. Take it easy, do some every day if you can. However it is that you choose to exercise, being steady about it is better than pushing yourself too hard just once in a while. As in everything in life, "Easy does it." Exercise improves brain function, hypertension, digestion, energy levels, metabolism, circulation, heart function, lung function, muscle tone, and certainly mood disorders. So what's not to like?

Some exercise I did today is_____

_____

_____

_____

_____

_____

_____

DECEMBER 20

He is not the God of the dead, but of the living...
– Mark 12: 27

Be like a moth to the light. You know how they love the light so much that they bat away at the porch lights. Get outside as much as you can, even when it's cold. Cold weather never stopped us when we were children. We'd play for hours in our snowsuits, no matter how caked with snow those warm clothes got. As adults, some of us have grown wimpy and stay indoors too much. Being cooped up in those closed interiors with all that artificially heated air and trapped household chemicals is bad for our health and bad for our moods. We need fresh air, and we need to get outside. And we'll feel so energized and so much the better for it.

An achievement today is_____
_____
_____
_____
_____
_____
_____
_____

DECEMBER 21

...Beware of the scribes who like to walk around in long robes, and like respectful greetings in the marketplaces.

– Mark 12: 38

Remember as we approach Christmas, to enjoy the reason for the season. It's not about getting frazzled over all those presents you're worried about. Enjoy the spirit of Christmas and remember that Jesus was a carpenter. Maybe in honor of his working with His hands, you can make gifts for those people on your list. Handmade presents done with love and care mean much more than something you ran out and frantically bought. We can take pride in whatever it is we make to give away. Going in debt to celebrate a commercial Christmas is not what Jesus would have wanted for the season celebrating His birth. Don't let the pressures of our consumer oriented society weigh on you. Love, light, and peace are much more important than all the Christmas shopping madness.

An achievement today is_____

_____

_____

_____

DECEMBER 22

...Why is it that you were looking for Me? Did you not know that I had to be in My Father's house?

– Luke 2: 49

The more we practice our coping skills, the better we get at it. One of the techniques for maintaining our balance during the hectic days during the holidays is to make time for quiet time in the morning. A time when you can refresh yourself and prepare for the day by listening to your inner guidance. It's been said many times that the busier we are, the more important it is to take that quiet time to listen for direction. And, when faced with a choice, remember to ask yourself: *Which choice will move me further toward God, and which choice will move me away from God?*

Inner guidance I heard today is_____

_____

_____

_____

_____

_____

_____

_____

DECEMBER 23

...It is written, 'Man shall not live on bread alone.'
– Luke 4: 4

During the winter, I bake bread every week. One of the breads I make regularly uses a basic yeast bread recipe to which I add pumpkin from a can, (or fresh if I have any left from the garden), raisins, pecans, and cinnamon. Sometimes I use a bit of sugar, often I leave it out. I use pecans because I have a great many pecan trees on the farm. I call this pumpkin/pecan bread, and it has a golden color to it. You can cut back on whatever oil is called for in your bread recipe because of the pumpkin. Baking therapy is calming, and the smell of baking bread in the house is also calming, especially during the holidays. Remember that the longer you knead yeast bread, the finer will be the texture. Knead it until it's smooth as satin, and watch your mood improve all the while with this hands-on work.

An achievement today is_____

_____

_____

_____

DECEMBER 24

…Why are you reasoning in your hearts?

– Luke 5: 22

Living in Cajun country as I do, I always look forward to the Cajun tradition of serving seafood gumbo on Christmas Eve. However, my favorite Christmas Eve was the night my mother and I walked home to our Pennsylvania farm from Stockertown, a small town just a few miles down the road. That particular night was so beautiful with sparkling snow on the ground, creaking ice on the branches of the trees along the fields, and an abundance of stars in the clear night sky. We heard bells playing *Silent Night, Holy Night* from the town, and the scene remains vividly in my mind all these years later. That night has always been the quintessential Christmas Eve for me.

My most memorable Christmas memory is _____

_____

_____

_____

_____

_____

_____

_____

DECEMBER 25

Be glad in that day and leap for joy...
– Luke 6: 23

Christmas can be a happy day for many. But, for many, it can be a sad, even forlorn day. Those who have lost their families, or who have hit on hard times, or who are far from home, or who have sad memories of Christmas days gone by, may not look forward to, or even enjoy Christmas day. If you know anyone like that, you might invite them along to do something fun. There are long lines at the movies on the holidays, for example. Or you may want to volunteer to help serve dinners at the Salvation Army, or another helping organization.

The best thing that happened today is_____

_____

_____

_____

_____

_____

_____

_____

_____

_____

DECEMBER 26

There is another who testifies of Me, and I know that the testimony which He gives about Me is true.

–John 5: 32

The English call the day after Christmas, Boxing Day. As we clear away the wrappings, we can use it as a metaphor for clearing away anything else we want to let go of from the past year. We're preparing for a new year, and new revelations and insights. We await the New Year with expectations for the many beautiful things we will observe, and the many blessings we are bound to receive. We leave behind anything that detracts and distracts from our peace and serenity.

Something I am letting go of is_____

_____

_____

_____

_____

_____

_____

_____

_____

_____

DECEMBER 27

…Go; it shall be done for you as you have believed…
– Matthew 8: 13

If it's cold where you are, focus on the warm shining light that shines within your spirit. You can move it around too. For example, if you discover it in your core, you can move it elsewhere in your body, simply by focusing it there. If it's cold, keep your head covered because much heat leaves the body through the crown of our head. And as for socks! I'm never without my socks in the wintertime! Keep expanding that inner warmth until it fills your body. You really can do this. Shirley Maclaine talked about doing this one night when she was bitter cold while high in the Andes. It worked for her, and it can work for us also.

An achievement today is_____

_____

_____

_____

_____

_____

_____

DECEMBER 28

By your endurance you will gain your lives.

– Luke 21: 19

Remember the acronym KISS? Keep it simple, Sweetheart? The more we simplify our life, the lighter our moods will be. Less is more. Ask yourself each time you want to buy something….Can I do without that? I'm one of those people who won't get rid of something if it still works. My daughter wanted me to buy a new refrigerator when she visited. She likes the new styles. However, mine kept my freezer food frozen throughout five days of no electric power in the aftermath of a hurricane. So why would I ditch it after such a performance? But then, I'm one of the few people left in the deep South who doesn't use air conditioning. Just ceiling fans and open windows. Anyhow, I *really* believe in keeping it simple. It's a whole lot easier that way. And simplicity is good for our moods.

Something I can do to simplify my life is_____

_____

_____

_____

_____

_____

_____

DECEMBER 29

But no one can enter the strong man's house and plunder his property unless he first binds the strong man...

– Mark 3: 27

As the year draws to a close, remember that the best things in life often come out of the worst things in life. So, if you had a bad time in the past year, look for the good that is going to come out of it. And if you lost something, remember ...if you're supposed to have it, you'll get it back in one form or another. And probably in a way you would never expect. So keep looking out for the good things that are going to come your way in the New Year. And cast the old year under the silvery light of a mist or fog. It's almost over. I can hear some of you saying, "Thank God!"

An achievement today is_____

_____

_____

_____

_____

_____

_____

_____

_____

DECEMBER 30

...I am He...

– John 18: 5

If one of your loved ones is struggling with alcohol or drugs this season...(the holidays can be a hard time for addictive personalities)...get to an Al-Anon meeting. Al-Anon's effectiveness and support is widely recognized. If no one near you has an addiction problem that is affecting your life, remember about Al-Anon in case you may want to refer a friend who is upset because of a loved one's addictions.

An achievement today is_____

_____
_____
_____
_____
_____
_____
_____
_____
_____
_____

DECEMBER 31

...and he who does not take his cross and follow after Me is not worthy of Me.

– Matthew 10: 38

As we ask in prayer for help with any depressed mood we may be struggling with, we know we can do this at any time during the day or night. If we care to keep a prayer journal, recording what we prayed about and when, we can look back and see just what has transpired since praying over a matter. If we face a perplexing situation, we can pray about that. If we are up against a difficult decision, we can pray over that as well. Or, we can remain silent and listen for guidance. That is prayer as well. (This is my favorite way of praying, because I have learned to respect the saying: *There are more tears shed over answered prayers, than unanswered ones.*) Congratulations! You've made it through another year!

My prayer for the New Year is_____

_____

_____

_____

_____

_____

22010745R00216

Made in the USA
Lexington, KY
08 April 2013